SOCIAL
CONNECTIONS

Consistently Connect with and Engage Your Aud

JASON CASTON

http://tenconnections.com

http://twitter.com/tenconnections

2015 Edition – v1

Caston Digital Books

Copyright © 2015 by Caston Digital, LLC

ISBN-10: 0985787333

ISBN-13: 978-0-9857873-3-2

Written By: Jason Caston

Cover Design: ArtisticEmbodiment.com – Twitter: @CB_Artistic1

Dedication

This book is dedicated to my dear family and friends. Thanks for continually lifting me up and helping me reach new heights. Your encouragement is always appreciated!

Technology Disclaimer

I will update this book as often as possible to stay current with the most recent technologies. I will also keep the latest version in print and make it available via the TenConnections.com website. Thanks, and I hope this book is beneficial to you and your organization.

Table of Contents

Introduction

In January 2010, I became the Social Media manager for an international nonprofit organization. The Facebook fan page and Twitter accounts didn't exist, and the organization wasn't really interested in Social Media. Now, fast-forward to October 2012. The Facebook Fan page hit 1 Million fans. By May 2013, the Twitter page hit 1 Million followers and we were off and running.

This type of success was no accident. It was very intentional. The tipping point came when the organization did three things in October 2010: It developed a Social Media team and strategy; integrated Social Media into their external marketing; and convinced the CEO to get more active in Social Media. As the audience grew, we realized how important Social Media was and how it could become a significant part of the marketing and overall strategy of the organization.

After this type of success, it was time to help others learn how to best use Social Media and achieve these results. Thus, *Social Connections* was written. Developed by me, *Social Connections* is a book of strategies and methods used to effectively connect with and engage your audience.

Goals of this Book

The goals of this book include…

- Setting a realistic expectation that, while gaining large numbers of fans is a great accomplishment, it is the quality of the engagement that is most important. ***Quality over Quantity*** should be the focus. From there, we will build toward the result of greater numbers.

- Giving you actual strategies to use on each network. These strategies will increase engagement and open new lines of communication between your organization and online followers.

- Emphasizing the necessity a content strategy while helping you develop one. Content Strategy is more important than anything else we will discuss in this book. Without great content, Social Media is useless.

- Explaining our overall Social Media strategy and how we utilize inspiration/education, information, communication, diversification and consistency.

- Explaining how to seize the moment and take advantage of Social Media moments.

- Highlighting the benefits and drawbacks of each social network.

- Relaying the fact that, even if you have one person handling your Social Media, or just a few, there must be a way to manage it all.

- Engagement is key in social media, it's "social" media for a reason.

What is Social Media?

Just as organizations were getting comfortable with the Internet and how they "thought" we should use it, Social Media transformed the Internet and gave these organizations larger platforms and more power to communicate with the world. We can, now, reach all the corners of the globe from our organizations' connected devices. Of course, we all know the adage, "With great power comes great responsibility." Social Media is no exception.

Social Media is one of the best ways to reach people with your message. Via their choice of social network, you can reach people right where they are by allowing the information to flow from your organization to their social profile. Businesses should strive to reach people wherever they are, on whatever network their audience chooses, via any device with which they connect. This is the opportunity social networks give us.

Social Media is a broad topic with a broad range of explanations. Numerous people have branded themselves as Social Media experts. If you did a search for Social Media on Google, you would find millions of websites with different explanations for this growing topic. With this book, my goal is to give you a general understanding of Social Media in the broadest sense and offer specific explanations on how to use it for the benefit of your organization. There are numerous statistics, facts, and definitions people quote when talking about Social Media. However, when it comes to Social Media, the consensus is simple: Connect with and engage your audience. In other words, *be social!*

Why is Social Media Important?

With information quickly spreading from one friend to another, your organization being the one controlling the information and message is a good thing. People will talk, no matter what. So, it is imperative for your organization to be involved and participate in the conversation. Also, Social Media is the simplest marketing channel an organization can use. A great organization should take advantage of this and have a social network outreach department that reaches people outside of your website, interacts with them, and brings them back to the website for more information. Now, we will discuss a few of the key reasons why Social Media is important.

- More People - Social Media reaches far more people than anything else out there. The key feature with Facebook is that a posting of content on Person A's page (wall) alerts all of his friends to the new information and sends some or all of that new information to these friends. It is a like a mass email without you having to take any action, other than posting content on your Facebook page. When Person A's friends receive this "mass email," they can spread it to their friends, which is likely a different group than Person A's friends. This process goes on and on, especially with compelling content. Have you heard the phrase, "Going viral"? Compelling content can spread so fast on Social Media that computer servers often shutdown due to a high volume of traffic.

- Interactive - Another reason why Social Media is critical is its interactive nature. Being able to have and maintain a two-way conversation allows for numerous possibilities. Is someone thinking about purchasing your product? Are they considering attending your

10

event? Social Media allows for instant responses and continued communication with relevant content, such as video, photos, and podcasts. The immediacy of the connection must be emphasized. If a staff member is assigned to this task, they will be able to respond faster, which significantly increases the chances of helping the other person.

- <u>Direct Connection and Access</u> - Access to leadership is important to many customers. Social Media allows for this to happen. Company leadership can decide how they will connect to customers and what information they will receive. Social Media also allows for simple and effective connections to organizations, which provides greater interest, participation, and financial support.

- <u>Branding</u> - Using Social Media networks to get the word out about your organization allows you to brand it. Branding is important because it helps people understand what your organization stands for. It also aids in garnering greater participation in organization events and increased support. Another benefit of branding is the sale of more products as people connect with your brand more intimately. Many books have been written on the importance of branding. With Social Media, you can create and maintain your brand.

- <u>eCommerce</u> - Social Media networks make it easy to add eCommerce and, as a result, generate online revenue through donations. Displaying the progress of the latest fundraising goals can turn these online users into online givers. To sell products, online stores can be set up and integrated with Social Media to generate more revenue and, of course, add a greater presence.

- Research - Social Media is an excellent tool for engaging customers in a dialogue and receiving their input on particular issues. Because it is easy to give feedback, users have a higher rate of participation in questionnaires and quality control surveys. If your organization is trying to decide on a particular matter, creating a survey on a Social Media site will provide all the feedback and opinions you need to reach a decision.

- Customer Retention/Service – The ability to answer questions from your customers and online users creates a high satisfaction rating. This, in turn, maintains a higher retention rate for your organization. Using Social Media to address your customer's issue before it becomes a big problem is critical, because Social Media can spread negative information as fast as it spreads positive information!

- Lead Generation - Social Media allows your organization to actively seek out new customers by searching through tweets and Facebook pages to find who has mentioned your brand and who is having an issue that your products can resolve. Promotions are another way you can bring in new customers, and promotions are easy to set up on a Social Media site.

- <u>Share Everything!</u> – Sharing everything doesn't necessarily mean pulling back the veil and letting everyone into every aspect of your organization. Nevertheless, there are two important concepts of sharing that Social Media provides. First, share as much content as possible via your social networks. Share daily information, weekly events, products, leadership updates, photos, videos, blogs, and everything else you can think of that would be of interest to current customers, potential customers, and online supporters. This continuous flow of fresh content keeps your social networks vibrant while giving your online users a ton of relevant information to consume and re-share. Second, make as much content shareable as possible. When you post content to your social networks, it should automatically be shareable by the networks. When you post this content to your website, you can add Facebook "Like Buttons," Google "+1 Buttons," and "Sharethis" sharing links. This makes your content shareable. Therefore, no matter what a user is reading on your website, they can immediately share it with their networks.

Social Media Statistics

Now that we have a better understanding of Social Media, we will look at some amazing stats about Social Media and how it has transformed the way we communicate and use the Internet.

- Social Media is the #1 activity on the web: It has overtaken email, web surfing, and pornography.
- Facebook is the #1 Social Network in 130 out of 137 countries around the world.

- Facebook has over 1.3 billion users. If it were a country, it would be the 3rd largest country in the world.

- YouTube has +1 billion unique viewers per month.

- Twitter has +500 million users (283 million active).

- Google+ has 1 billion users (90 million active).

- LinkedIn has +261 million users.

- Instagram clocks in with +300 million users.

- Pinterest is no slouch with +70 million users.

- 71% of Social Media users access it from a mobile device.

- The average Facebook user has 338 friends.

- Monthly active users on Facebook are 850 million.

- 488 million people regularly use Facebook via their mobile device.

- 60 million photos are uploaded to Instagram every day.

- The average Twitter user has tweeted 307 times.

- The average Twitter user is followed by 208 people.

- 56% of customer tweets to brands are ignored.

- There are 175 million tweets sent every day, ***and that number is growing***.

- 50% of Twitter users are mobile.

- Generations Y and Z consider email passé. They communicate via SMS and Social Media only.

- Many colleges are no longer distributing email accounts. Instead, they are communicating with their students via Social Media.

- Social Gamers are predicted to buy $6 billion worth of virtual goods this year.
- 90% of consumers trust peer recommendations via Social Media.
- Every minute, 100 hours of video content is uploaded to YouTube.
- 53% of people on Twitter recommend products in their tweets.

The Rise of Visual Social Media

When we were young, our introduction to learning was visual with items such as large picture books and cartoon videos. As we grew older, we moved away from the visual and more towards text-based content. Textbooks in schools are a great example of this. Social Media was the exact opposite of this. It started with text-based chat, email, and browsers that weren't aesthetically pleasing. Over the last few years, however, Social Media has entered a new stage of growth and focused on "visual content" that can be created, consumed, and easily shared. This is one of the main keys to building a large fan base, as well as communicating with them. By providing engaging visual content, you will ignite them into action. Photos, graphics, and videos are a great example of this.

Facebook first exhibited this phenomenon when it introduced its "Timeline" feature. Timeline effectively transformed a user's Facebook profile into a visual representation of their Facebook existence. Additionally, Facebook allowed users to start adding events, past locations, and milestones to their Facebook profiles. Now, this profile page not only became a visual representation of a user's online life, but their offline life too! Facebook also started filtering a user's newsfeed to provide customized content based on the top 30% - 40% of people a user interacted with most. In order to get more people to interact with the user and see their posts, they had to be more visual in nature, specifically with photos, videos, and graphics, because these could be shared and consumed easily from any device.

When Twitter added the ability to share photos and videos without having to use outside services, it was a clear sign that Twitter realized the importance of visual features. Then, Twitter added a cover photo and photo album feature on the user's profile page where people could see all the photos they uploaded to Twitter. This was yet another visual feature that pulled people to their site, made them stay longer, and gave them more reasons to share photos on Twitter.

Google+ has also focused on "visual content" within their social network by recently adding quite a few features. The large cover photo that each profile page has is a great example. It is the first thing you see when you go to a person's or business's Google+ page. Google+ has also updated their photo albums with larger viewing options and full-sized photo uploads. Larger photos hold people's attention longer and increases engagement. The option for full-size uploads allows people to keep their entire photo albums within Google+. Additionally, Google+ highlights and expands photos and videos in the stream so they stand out while people are viewing them, thus drawing the user's attention more quickly, especially on mobile devices. If that was not enough, Google+ is heavily integrated into YouTube.

YouTube, the #1 video site on the entire Internet, has always been one of the most visual social networks. Unfortunately, not until recently did people consider it a social network in addition to a video destination. YouTube has continued to enhance its video viewing features, commenting features, and a host of other features that continue to make this video platform the best on the Internet.

More recently, we have seen the rise of platforms like Pinterest, Vine, Snapchat, Tumblr, and Instagram. Each of them is a fully visual social network that is built on photos and videos. Instagram has become the #1 mobile photo-sharing application, and the video feature is growing significantly in usage. The best part about Instagram is that it is completely mobile, which displays the power of mobile photo/video sharing. Likewise, Pinterest was initially thought to be only a photo-sharing sight for women and moms. However, as Pinterest's popularity has exploded, it is more than just a network for photos. Their secret is that they also accept videos. This multimedia social network lets people "pin" photos and videos expressing themselves and their brands in full multimedia fashion. Vine and its six-second videos have grown in popularity, thereby attracting large audiences that constantly consume short videos, comment on them, like them, and share ("revine") them with their friends. And, we cannot simply forget Snapchat and their visual content (video and photos) that are shown for a set period of time and then expire. (Disclaimer: "Expire" merely means removed from view on the app, not removed from their servers or removed from the Internet. Do not believe that this digital content is gone forever. *Nothing* put on the Internet is gone forever…*NOTHING.*) Snapchat has become very popular amongst the younger demographic, and they are creating an enormous amount of multimedia content, and sharing it on-the-go.

The Impact of Mobile Social Media

Just as important as "Visual Social Media" is the impact of "Mobile Social Media." When Social Media first became popular, it was Myspace that ushered in this new way of communicating. Myspace gave us custom URL's, and we were able to connect with numerous people on the platform. We even had the opportunity to highlight our top 8 friends and let everyone know who was at the top of our friends list. When Facebook came onto the scene, there was no mass migration to it, until they implemented a feature that changed Social Media as we know it. They made the website mobile-compatible, and they released apps on all the major mobile platforms. This feature was something that Myspace couldn't match, and the convenience of being able to socially communicate on-the-go became one of the major parts of Facebook's early success and the demise of Myspace. Also, please remember that Facebook bought Instagram for $1 billion simply because its increasingly large following and that it was a great photo-based mobile platform.

Twitter followed this same route as they made sure their platform was mobile-focused. The 140-character messages that are the main focus of tweets is based on text messages being limited to 140 characters on mobile phones. Twitter wanted to make sure their messages would be delivered within a single text on mobile devices. Their mobile-first approach has led to their platform being one of the go-to sources for up-to-the-minute breaking news around the world.

Vine and their fully mobile six-second video platform, Snapchat with their mobile platform, YouTube's mobile app, Pinterest's mobile app, Tumblr's mobile app, and Linkedin's mobile app all show their understanding of how important mobile Social Media is and its unlimited potential for growth.

Mobile Social Media is growing significantly, and here are a few key mobile Social Media statistics:

- 2x more sharing happens via mobile as opposed to desktop.
- 71% of people use Social Media from their mobile device.
- 76% of Twitter access is mobile.
- 50% of Tumblr content is accessed via mobile.
- 40% of YouTube Access is mobile.
- 68% of Facebook Access is mobile.
- Mobile devices will increasingly play an important role, considering more than 60% of the population accesses Social Media content using them.
- Mobile Video will become more popular than photos.
- 94% of the marketing executives that have invested in mobile ads considered themselves satisfied with the results of using this tactic.
- This year, there has been an increase from 33% to 38% in the use of mobile marketing by various enterprises.

We are Just a Small Organization. What Can We Do?

"We are just a small organization. Social Media is so overwhelming." If I were to count how many times I have heard that statement, I would be busy for the next 5 years! Yes, I do agree that Social Media can be overwhelming. Even still, you have to start somewhere! When the organization I work for began using Social Media, our goal was to provide a good mix of "social" and "media." We wanted to make sure we were "social" and interacted with our online users while providing "media" through a steady flow of high-quality content from our organization. The success we had was amazing. Now, let's be clear. It was due to a strategy that we put into action daily. Later in this book, I will give you specifics on what to post, what times to post, and what types of content to post. Remember, if you tell your story visually and authentically, the people you are trying to reach will subscribe, like, and follow you and engage with you through your chosen Social Media platforms. These strategies will help you learn how to build your audience, increase interaction, and reach numerous fans.

Another key step in building your Social Media following is to integrate it with your offline marketing. Here are some examples you can begin using now:

- Add Social Media *sharing features* to your website and allow people to share with their Social Media networks.
- Add Social Media *follow icons* to your website and high-traffic webpages. This allows people to follow your organization from the pages they visit often.
- Add Social Media to all of your marketing materials. This includes, but is not limited to, fliers, ads, and print publications. You want your Social Media information on everything your organization puts out.

- Have the CEO/Pastor buy into and use Social Media. Then, get your employees on board. Make Social Media a significant part of the entire online marketing strategy.
- If you have online video, add *#hashtags* and *@twittername* to the broadcast so people can communicate with their social network about what they are watching online or on TV.

No organization starts out with a large online following. We all begin with a few and work our way up. *Or, do we?*

Should Your Organization Buy Followers/Views/Fans/Retweets?

Late Summer 2012, Mitt Romney's Twitter followers increased by 100,000 in a matter of days, and quite a few people took notice. Unfortunately, there wasn't a specific public event that made his Twitter count jump. So, people wondered how it was possible. Well, this event shed light on a new opportunity that arose for Social Media marketing companies. I speak of fake followers, views, fans, and retweets. There are companies that sell Twitter followers and retweets, YouTube Subscribers and views, Facebook Fans, Pinterest Followers and Repins, and Instagram Followers and Likes. These companies give organizations the illusion of high Social Media numbers without having a legitimate following. Therefore, a new question must be asked: Should your organization purchase fans, followers, retweets, and views from these companies? Well, yes and no.

The answer is *yes* if you are merely trying to get your Social Media numbers up for appearance's sake. If your organization has numerous followers and wants even higher numbers because it believes that will lead more people to follow you, then, by all means, yes.

The answer is *no* if you are looking to actually have interaction, communication, and engagement with your Social Media followers. If you want to actually *participate* in the "social" aspect of Social Media, you must have a strategy that will detail how you will distribute and interact with people. In other words, if you want followers, likes, retweets, fans, views, and repins, earn them!

The real question is, "What does your organization want from Social Media?"

Which Network is the Best?

Is it Facebook and their one billion users? Is it Twitter and their easy-to-use network? Is it Instagram/Pinterest and their Pictures and Videos? Is it YouTube and their massive video network? Which one is it? My friend, the answer is simple: The best social network is whichever one your organization knows how to use. This is the hardest part for organizations to grasp when they embark upon using Social Media. Simply begin with the network your staff knows best. Consider the following four points:

1. The social network your organization should use depends on your content and your capability to use the network. If you have only a small amount of content consisting of a

few photos, text updates, and videos, and the people you have on staff know Twitter best, you should get going on Twitter. If you have people on staff familiar with Facebook, use that social network to push text, video, and photo updates. Use whatever network your content will work on and the one with which your people are familiar.

2. Repurpose your content for each network. Once you have decided to use more than one network, you can repurpose the same content for multiple networks. For example, if you have a motivational quote from your Pastor's sermon, you can take that quote and post it on Facebook, Twitter, Tumblr, and Google+. Then, you can take the quote, use it in a picture/meme of your Pastor preaching, and upload it to Facebook, Twitter, Google+, Instagram, Snapchat, Tumblr, and Pinterest. Also, you can use the actual video of your Pastor saying the same quote, and post that video clip to Facebook, Twitter, Google+, Pinterest, Tumblr, Vine, Snapchat, and YouTube. As you can see, different types of the same content can go on different networks.

3. Each network has its own community and its own best way to use it. For the sake of time, many organizations will have their Facebook posts go to Twitter, or the other way around. While this conserves time, it takes away from the uniqueness of each network and hinders genuine growth on the network to which content is being pushed. Usually, the network that has content being pushed to it is the one that is not being monitored. Therefore, people desiring to interact with the business on that network are not being

answered. That network is usually just something that is being fed content without anyone attending to it.

4. You don't have to be on every network, but it's good to be on as many as your staff can handle. If you can only be on one network, make the most of that network until you get the ability to expand to more.

<u>Social Media Strategy - What Strategy Should My Organization Have for Social Media?</u>

A CONSISTENT ONE! This is also one of the most difficult parts of using Social Media. Too many times a company will develop a strategy but find the time commitment to maintain that strategy is more than the staff has available. Another difficult hurdle to implementing a consistent strategy is producing content consistently. So, what can we do to set up a Social Media strategy that works?

First, take a good look at your staff and decide how much time they can devote to a Social Media strategy. *Be realistic.* Make sure you understand what tasks each person already performs and ensure these new responsibilities can fit into their time. Who will be the person that champions the Social Media networks, gathers the information from the rest of the business, and actually distributes the information to the networks? This person needs to have a good understanding of social networks and the benefits of one network over another.

The ideal situation would allow for organizations to hire Social Media managers who can communicate via the networks, develop campaigns, measure results, and deliver organized data on the progress of the company's networks. However, this person comes at a price. If this is out of the budget, utilize a young person that is very excited and energetic when it comes to Social Media. This person will not be afraid of new social networks and will enjoy sharing content and interacting on behalf of the business.

The next step is determining exactly who your audience is. Segment your audience into categories so that you can gather content geared towards a specific audience. For example, if you are targeting online users who are not familiar with your brand, tailor a Social Media post differently than if you are targeting online users who have already subscribed to your brand. Most brands say they are focusing on fans and non-fans, but their messages are always catered to fans only. This wastes a great opportunity to reach millions of other social networkers that may not be familiar with them just yet. Those users are ripe for the pick up! Social Media has the advantage of reaching people right where they are, speaking a message to them in a way they need to receive it, and moving them toward making necessary changes for the better.

After you have determined your audience, look at the content you currently generate. Social Media is an excellent tool to distribute repurposed content. Take a careful inventory of your weekly production of content. Then, make a list of how many different items your staff can produce. Content is king. Keep your audience engaged. If you have plenty of staff and time to post to Social Media sites, yet have poor or inconsistent content, the effectiveness of your strategy will be greatly diminished.

So, let's ask a few questions. What is your brand's message? What is the voice of your company? What is the message you wish to convey to people via Social Media? How will you communicate it? Will your organization speak on societal and current issues? Will your organization push out marketing updates and never respond to people? Make sure your organization isn't one-dimensional. There are many types of people you can reach, so you must distribute many types of Social Media posts in order to reach them. To give you some guidelines, here are four focal points in establishing your organization's message via Social Media:

- <u>Education/Inspiration</u> - Make sure to provide education, inspiration, and motivation via your social networks. These are the best types of posts. Whether they are quotes, photos with encouraging words on them, or quick videos that give educational tips about your organization or industry, everyone wants content that enhances their lives.

- <u>Information</u> - Provide information about your organization by using your social networks. Please do not assume everyone reads your website or even saw your eblast. Distribute the information about events and other happenings through those same social networks. You can also repurpose flyers, newsletters, eblasts, and other marketing materials and send them out.

- <u>Communication</u> - Social Media is *social*! Therefore, it should be a two-way communication. If you post to a network and people comment, ask questions, and take time out of their busy day to respond, make sure your organization takes time to acknowledge them and respond back. Do not appear too arrogant to respond to your social network fans, even if you do not have the staff or time to answer every comment or question. At least answer some. Show that the organization sees their comments and questions and cares about their audience's concerns.

- <u>Consistency</u> - Make sure the content from your organization flows consistently from your online properties to your online users. On some networks, this means posting multiple times a day or once a week. It depends on the network. That being said, no matter which one your organization uses, you must maintain consistency.

- <u>Diversification</u> – Have you noticed that neither Social Media network has been mentioned to be better than another? The network you use to distribute content to your online users is irrelevant if there is no consistent strategy behind it. Ten years ago, everyone was using AOL email to communicate with the masses. Five years ago, it was MySpace. Three years ago, Facebook and Twitter became popular. Just recently, Instagram, Vine, and Snapchat have become very prevalent. The networks will come and go. So, do not make the mistake of putting all your eggs in one Social Media basket. Find a network you want to use and grow on it. Then, add another network and repeat. You do not have to be present on all the social networks that are out there. Simply don't depend on just one network to be your savior.

How to Manage it All

The first question an organization needs to answer is, "How many people will participate in the Social Media strategy?" A good recommendation is that you start out with two people and see how it goes. The reason behind two people is that one person should be in charge of gathering content while the other person is in charge of pushing it out. Of course, you can have more people do this because you may want to have a collection of people commenting and responding to users on the social networks. Initially, the main focus should be gathering content and distributing it.

- How many hours per day? – Social Media operates 24 hours a day. However, it's unrealistic to believe someone will be managing your properties 24 hours a day. Instead, dedicate 2 – 4 hours a day to gathering content, scheduling it for social networks, and responding to online users. As time progresses, and you get more people involved, you will increase those hours. By that time, hopefully, your process will be much more streamlined.

- <u>Native vs. 3rd-party Posting</u> – There has been a new debate raging for the last few years ever since Facebook started tweaking their algorithm and limiting how many people could see a post. When Facebook started limiting how many of our friends' posts we were seeing in our newsfeed (you normally see 30% - 40% of your friends' posts and pages you liked in your newsfeed), people started to look at different ways they could increase their presence and get into more users' newsfeeds. Likewise, when businesses and brands saw their posts were only being seen by an average of 4% of their audience, they immediately wanted to know of ways to reach more of them (outside of the promoted posts and advertising options that I will discuss later). HootSuite.com and other online software that helped these companies manage their Social Media channels were considered a solution, until a rumor started floating around that Facebook was limiting the reach (how many people) of the posts (adding videos, photos, status updates) coming from 3rd-party software. This led to an interesting debate as to whether you should use 3rd-party software to manage your Social Media channels or post natively. Posting natively means to post from within the actual Social Media network itself. The solution has been mixed and some people say that 3rd-party software tools work better, and others say native postings work better. Facebook has even issued a statement that 3rd-party tools would not be limited in their reach. Based on personal usage and published statistics, I discovered that each network favors native usage over 3rd-party usage. A great example is the native photo and video features of Facebook and Twitter. Both of these networks favor their native posting features over 3rd-party solutions. Facebook will show a video posted directly to their network to many more people instead

29

of a link to a YouTube video. Therefore, while it is easier and less time-consuming to use HootSuite, Buffer, and other Social Media management tools to do your work for you, native posting gets the best results on each network.

- <u>Software to Help</u> – Even though possible reach issues with 3rd-party software were just mentioned, it is still necessary to cover a few of them. After all, they are extremely helpful and valuable. There are many good ones that I use consistently. They include HootSuite.com, Bufferapp.com, and Sproutsocial.com. HootSuite and Buffer are free scheduling software that make Social Media management much easier. They also connect with social networks such as Facebook, Twitter, Google+, and LinkedIn and allow you to schedule updates, add photos, and links. You can do all this and still coordinate a full Social Media strategy from one location. The main benefit of HootSuite and Buffer is that you can schedule out all your Facebook, LinkedIn, Google+, and Twitter posts for the week (or month) at one time and let the software automatically post items for you. This will keep a continuous stream of content flowing, thus allowing you to focus on other things like gathering more content and responding to online users from various social networks. HootSuite also has great reporting features that can help you identify some key metrics in your Social Media campaign. Have you ever wanted to know your top 10 followers? How about how many people clicked the link you sent out? Are you thinking about how many people "like" you on a weekly basis on social networks? HootSuite has those answers for you.

Add this capability in with the features of Sprout Social and Google Analytics, and you can see how effective your Social Media campaigns are performing on a grand scale.

How to use HootSuite.com

To setup your account, visit www.hootsuite.com and enter your email, full name, and password. Click the "Sign Up Now" button, and that should be it. The free version of HootSuite allows you to manage 5 different Social Media accounts simultaneously. If you want to manage unlimited accounts, you can browse other plans under "Plans and pricing."

To begin importing your social accounts, first, login to HootSuite using the same email address and password you used to create your account. From there, you can see it is really simple to add your Twitter, Facebook, and LinkedIn accounts. HootSuite can share and post information to your Facebook, LinkedIn, and Twitter Profile on your behalf, once you accept the terms and conditions.

How to Use HootSuite to Schedule your Social Activity and Send Messages, and Add a Social Account

If you do not wish your composed messages to go out immediately, you have the option to decide on a future publishing date. All you have to do is click the "Calendar" button on your dashboard. Choose a desired date from the calendar, and click "Schedule." You can also click the "check" box next to "Email me when message is sent" to receive a notification when your message is posted.

Did you know that you can send your message to multiple social networks listed in your HootSuite account? Simply create a message. Then, select multiple profiles from the dialog box as highlighted in the figure below. As mentioned earlier, you can click the "Calendar" button and schedule your message. Once you have finished composing your message, click "Send Now" from the dialog box that appears on your screen.

To add a new social network to HootSuite, click the "Add Social Network" button on your dashboard and follow the instructions that appear on your screen. If you use Chrome or Firefox as your web browser, you can easily manage your HootSuite account with Hootlet.

Bufferapp.com

Buffer helps you concurrently manage multiple Social Media accounts. Quickly schedule content from anywhere on the web, collaborate with team members, and analyze rich statistics on how your posts perform. The best feature that makes Buffer one of the top Social Media management platforms is its sharing integration with websites and web browsers. While reading blogs and websites, you will see sharing options that allow you to share to Twitter, Facebook, LinkedIn, Google+, Email, and Buffer. Buffer has established itself as a wonderful option to use when reading content on the web and sharing it quickly with friends. Likewise, the Buffer plugin available for Google Chrome and Firefox gives the option to share any website being viewed while using those browsers. This browser plugin compliments the Buffer Mobile app that allows on-the-go sharing.

How to use Bufferapp.com

To set up an account on Buffer, visit bufferapp.com and choose which method you want to use to sign in. The choices are Twitter, Facebook, Linkedin, and Email. Once you choose your method, you are able to commence using the software on their limited "Free" plan. Consider how many Social Media accounts you are going to add to this software. The *Free Plan* allows for only a few accounts to be added. Upgrading to the *Awesome Plan* ($9.99 month) will allow you to add 15 RSS feeds, 10 Social Media accounts, and 100 posts and tweets in your Buffer queue (content waiting to post). If you need additional accounts, you can further upgrade to the *Business Plan*, which allows for more posting and accounts, but has higher monthly fees.

- Accounts - The first to-do on the list when you begin using Buffer is to add Social Media accounts. You will need to login to these accounts, preferably in the same web browser into which you are signed in to Buffer. Once you click on the "Accounts" option, you will be able to choose which account (Facebook, Twitter, LinkedIn, or Google+) you want to add. Once you click on the account, you will be asked to login to that account and confirm a few things, and it will be added to your account. Repeat this process until you have added all the necessary accounts.

- Content - This is an important tab because it is where you can see the content in your Buffer queue that you have added and what time it will post. As you continue adding content to your Buffer queue, you will see the Buffer queue tab continue to fill. If you cannot find content to add, you can use the "Suggestions" tab next to the queue. This tab gives ready-to-post content suggestions for you to add to your Buffer queue. If you have the premium features, you can use the "Contributions" tab, which shows team members and how they contributed various pieces of content to the queue. Lastly, the "Feeds" tab allows you to take a RSS feed and send the posted content right to your queue and out to your audience.

- Analytics - The "Analytics" tab gives you insight into how your posts are doing. From this tab, you can see what you have recently posted and how popular or unpopular those posts were. From here, you can use the additional premium tabs, "Analysis" and "Insights," that will give you a more in-depth look at your posts and how you can increase engagement, reach, and interaction.

- Schedule - This tab is where you create your posting schedule and set the frequency and times you want your content to post. You can choose any time of any day and add that to your schedule. Make sure you choose the correct time zone so that your posts are scheduled correctly based on your location. Once this schedule is set, when posts are added to the Buffer queue, they will automatically adhere to the scheduled day and times set in this tab.

- Settings – "Settings" has a variety of features, such as link shortening for link tracking, team member management, reconnecting social networks that may not be working correctly, and the ability to empty a network's queue.

Overall, Buffer is a great platform for Social Media management, and has a great interface and simple, useful layout. With it's competitive pricing, it is awesome software to employ in your Social Media strategy.

SproutSocial.com

Sprout Social is a Social Media management system (SMMS) with functionality for multiple-person teams and a focus on engagement, publishing, and analytics. Sprout's platform currently offers users the ability to integrate with Facebook, Twitter, Google+, LinkedIn, Zendesk, and UserVoice. Sproutsocial has the posting feature that Hootsuite and Buffer have, but that is not where this software shines. This software has some of the most in-depth analytics for the major Social Media platforms. This is a paid service, but you can sign up for a free trial to see if the service will work for your Social Media strategy.

How to use SproutSocial.com

To get started, go to SproutSocial.com and set up a new account. Once your account is set up, your first step is to decide *how* you want to set up your account. At the top right corner of the home page are buttons for groups, profiles, team members, and account settings. Each of these options helps you customize your software for your Social Media management. With the "Groups" option, you can specify which group your Social Media accounts will go under. If you have multiple brands or clients that you manage, you can create multiple groups for management.

You can specify which Social Media profiles will be accessed within each group. To add your Social Media feeds to the software, go to the home screen, click on the "+" button at the top right corner of the page, and choose which account you want to add. You may choose from Twitter, Facebook, Google+, or LinkedIn. After adding your desired accounts, the software will start measuring analytics. Within a day or so, you will have a wonderful snapshot of your Social Media platforms, engagement, and reach. The last major option for Sprout Social is "Team Members." This option allows you to add specific people to the account and specify the profiles and groups to which they have access. This option opens up the collaboration features where multiple people can work together on posting, analytics, and managing the Social Media platforms of the group.

- Messages - The "Messages" tab is the location of the "Smart Inbox." Smart Inbox brings all of your messages from all of your social profiles into a single stream. One of the best features of Sprout Social is the ability to take all of the platforms that are added to its software and give you a single place to communicate with your online fans.

- Tasks – This is the location of "Live Activity Updates" and a place to assign and manage tasks for team members. The "Activity Updates" feature allows everyone on the team to see who has responded to Social Media fans, as well as their completed activities. This feature is extremely useful in making sure there are no duplicate efforts in communicating while keeping an audit trail on who has done what. Also, the "Task" tab is where tasks are assigned and managed. With multiple team members working on Social Media accounts, this feature assists in managing efforts and ensuring the organization works smarter instead of harder.

- Feeds - The "Feeds" tab is a place to monitor RSS, Twitter, and Linkedin feeds. Once you connect these platforms to your account, you can choose which of these you would like to appear in your feed.

- Publishing - The "Publishing" tab is a place to post to multiple networks. Very similar to Hootsuite and Buffer, Sproutsocial has a scheduling option for multiple networks, including Facebook, Google+, Twitter, and Linkedin. The schedule, or "Team Content Calendar," can be viewed by all team members to keep them informed of what messages are being released daily and on which networks at whatever times. Also, the "Drafts" feature allows any team member to create a Social Media post and have it approved by senior team members prior to being posted to social networks. This system of approval helps protect individuals, as well as the messaging of the organization.

- Discovery - The "Discovery" tab gives you key people to follow, the silent accounts that are following you, and ways to cleanup your Social Media platforms for more optimized engagement. One of the key features of this tab is the "Key People to Follow" option. This gives you influencers that are following you, or are associated with your topics and would help expand your Social Media reach.

- Reports - The "Reports" tab is one of the most essential aspects of the entire Sprout Social software. Not only does this software give you in-depth reports with a wealth of data, such as hashtag monitoring, platform statistics, Social Media reach, social trends, and more, it also presents all of this in presentation-ready format. As you go through the reports tab and begin creating reports that will best help you "analyze, optimize, and repeat" your Social Media strategies, you will see how powerful this software truly is.

Best Times to Post

Another important question in your Social Media strategy that requires an answer is, "When am I supposed to post?" Since Social Media operates 24 hours a day, you cannot assume that all of your online users live only in your city, state or time zone. Therefore, you must adjust and adapt your strategy to a 24-hour schedule. This does not mean that someone has to be up at 2 a.m. posting for the organization. When using HootSuite.com, your content is already scheduled for posting. You can simply schedule overnight posts for people that may be on your social networks during late hours or on the other side of the world, where it's daytime. Here are some great example peak and nonpeak posting times:

Facebook
Daily Best Times: 1pm-4pm
Peak Time: Wednesday 3pm
Daily Worst Times: 8pm-8am

Twitter
Daily Best Times: 1pm-3pm
Peak Time: Mon-Thur 9am-3pm
Daily Worst Times: 8pm-9am

LinkedIn
Daily Best Times: 9am-9pm
Peak Time: 12pm or 5pm-6pm
Daily Worst Times: 10pm-6am or anytime Friday

Google+

Daily Best Times: 9am-11am

Peak Time: Wednesday 9am

Daily Worst Times: 6pm-8am

Pinterest

Daily Best Times: 2pm-4pm or 8pm-1am

Peak Time: Friday 3pm

Daily Worst Times: 5pm-7pm

Tumblr

Daily Best Times: Friday 7pm

Peak Time: Sun-Tues 7pm-10pm

Daily Worst Times: Before 4pm

*All times are in your local time zone

How Often to Post

How often to post is a question that many organizations face. How much is too much? Can we post 5 times a day? Should we post items twice in case people didn't see it the first time? These are questions that many organizations ask when they start using social networks. Here are some posting tips to keep in mind:

Facebook - Post at least 1-3 times a day

Twitter - Post at least 4-6 times a day

YouTube - Post at least 1 video per week

Pinterest - Post at least 1 photo per week

Instagram - Post at least 1 photo per week

Google+ - Post at least 1-3 times a day

Tumblr - Post at least 1-3 times a day

What to Post

Ranging from just plain text to a full video, we can publish just about any kind of content on our social networks and use it to reach the masses. With the rise in visual Social Media, we want to make sure we focus on a good mix of visual, engaging, and informative content. Visual content consists of mainly photos and videos, with photos becoming the most shared form of multimedia on the organizations. Listed below are the numerous types of content that we can distribute on Facebook, Twitter, Blogs/Tumblr, LinkedIn, Google+, YouTube, Instagram, Pinterest, and other social networks.

- Photos/Images/Graphics – Photos/images/graphics updates are one of the most popular uses of social networks. Since you can take pictures from 90% of smart phones these days, millions of people are taking photos and sharing them on their social networks. As of the last two years, photos are having the most significant impact on Social Media. They have become so important that Facebook paid $1 billion for Instagram, a network that only consists of sharing photos. Likewise, the photo-driven social network, Pinterest, has quickly become one of the fastest growing, most engaging social networks available today. For graphics, a more recent popular usage has emerged called "memes." A meme is a picture or image with words added to it that enhance the photo in some manner. The changes can be funny, motivational, and inspirational, or whatever you like. The point is they are shared more, get more comments, and engage users more online. Remember to only post images you own or have permission to post.

Networks to use for this type of content are Facebook, Instagram, Pinterest, Twitter, Snapchat, Google+, LinkedIn, and Blog/Tumblr.

- Video – Videos are the most engaging form of multimedia. They can be created on professional cameras or smartphone video cameras. Video is becoming a more popular form of multimedia on social networks due to popular video sharing networks like Instagram, Vine, SnapChat, Meerkat and YouTube Capture. These networks allow for quick recording, editing, and sharing of videos recorded from mobile devices. Once the video is recorded and edited, it can be uploaded to numerous Social Media websites.

Networks to use for this type of content are Facebook, YouTube, Pinterest, Instagram, Vine, Google+, SnapChat and Blog/Tumblr.

- Links – Links are simply clickable text. Once clicked, these links can take you to videos, documents, audio files, websites, images, or online posts, such as blogs.

  Networks to use for this type of content are Facebook, YouTube, Twitter, Google+, LinkedIn, and Blog/Tumblr.

- Statuses – A status update is an informational text-based update. Like Twitter and their limit of 140 characters, some social networking sites have character limits. Facebook and Google+ initially had character limits but have since lifted those limits.

  Networks to use for this type of content are Facebook, Twitter, Google+, LinkedIn, and Blog/Tumblr.

- Questions/Polls – Questions and Polls were originally just a status post that asked a question and waited for people to respond. Now, they are regularly used as part of a Social Media strategy.

  Networks to use for this type of content are Facebook, Twitter, Instagram, Vine, Google+, LinkedIn, and Blog/Tumblr.

- Events – In Facebook, you can setup events, invitations, and reminders to which people can RSVP online. This online "Events" feature provides the same functionality as Evite, allowing you to see who is coming to your event as well as letting people share and socialize about your event.

Networks to use for this type of content are Facebook and Google+.

- <u>Location-based strategies (check-in feature)</u> – The newest feature that has been quite popular is location-based social networking. Foursquare, Facebook, and Twitter have features that allow you to broadcast your location to your friends. Another option is the "Check-in" feature, which gives users the option to check-in to places with their mobile devices. In addition to broadcasting their location, they can receive online coupons and deals.

  Networks to use for this type of content are Facebook, Foursquare, and Google+.

Organizational Content You Should Post

Now that we have discussed the forms of content posting, we will talk about the specific organizational content you can post. Your organization produces a variety of content, and once you start to gather and repurpose it, you can distribute it through a variety of social networks. Here are some examples of great content that can be sent out on social networks.

- <u>Leadership Updates</u> – Videos, Blogs, and other quick updates can help your Social Media followers feel connected to the leadership. It does not have to be a professionally-produced video or an award-winning novel. Just give the users a way to connect with the CEO and/or leadership using their social networks.

- <u>Products</u> – Links to products in an online store can be sent out through social networks. Your online fans can, then, find out about sales, promotions, and other hot products the organization is offering.

- <u>Photos</u> – Make sure to distribute photos of activities, community work, and new staff members. There are a variety of things you can take pictures of and distribute via your social networks. So, make sure you keep those photos coming!

- <u>Daily Inspiration or Information</u> – Each day, people are looking for some type of hope, motivation and inspiration. Words of inspiration from your organization could start many followers' day off with hope and joy. You can also encourage them throughout the day with more posts.

- <u>Educational</u> – A great way to build an interactive online audience is to educate them. By providing educational content on your organization and/or industry, you will provide valuable content your audience desires. This will also help establish you and/or your organization as an expert in your area/industry.

- <u>Video clips from TV shows or events</u> – If your organization has a TV show that airs weekly, this is a good place to get great, engaging Social Media content. There are commercial video clips that could help increase awareness, interest, and viewership of the weekly show. In addition to showing the video clips of the TV show, you can broadcast the entire show online using vimeo.com or youtube.com. You may also add a custom landing page tab with a link to donate online during the show, if you are a nonprofit.

- Interactive Polls – In order to get online users talking and interacting with the Facebook fan page and other Social Media networks, weekly interactive polls and current events can be posted online. Results can be calculated instantly and shared among the Facebook fans.

- Digital Downloads – Find a digital download to give away as incentive for online users to join your Social Media account. Make it a very inspiring message that is selling well in the online store. This will make users feel like they are getting a high-value product.

Optimizing Your Posts

First and foremost, it cannot be overstated: When you post content through your networks, make sure you optimize it for interaction and sharing. The following are a few examples of how to do this.

- Call-to-Action - When you share content, provide a call-to-action, such as asking to like, comment, share, or retweet your post. A call-to-action allows people feel like they are participating with the organization. When your organization posts something engaging and moves someone to action, they make a conscious decision to participate in your Social Media marketing. This is the power of social networking. As your organization reciprocates that communication and engagement, the online relationship becomes deeper, which causes those fans to become self-proclaimed brand advocates and marketers. Make sure you place a call-to-action in your post and allow people to participate in your Social Media campaigns with you.

• Ask Questions – As you build your Social Media audience, "crowd-source" things you need to know by asking your online audience what they think. Ask them questions about your brand, current topics, new products, and other things that will give your organization pertinent information to help build your business. Marketing companies pay focus groups for information that you can get for FREE simply by using your Social Media networks. Another great reason to ask your online audience questions is that you can get immediate responses from REAL CUSTOMERS about your business, and that information is always valuable.

• Humor is helpful – Have you laughed today? Everyone wants to laugh, and studies have shown that people who laugh more live longer. Jokes, memes, stories, and humorous videos all grab attention and encourage your followers to be part of the conversation. There are two major things that occur when you post humorous content: (1) you get online viewers to stop, laugh, and spend time on your profiles, and (2) they are more likely to share the content with their friends.

- <u>Get Personal</u> – Your customers/fans want to know more about you. Many times, you are the brand—the key person people are looking to connect with. Therefore, get connected! Share stories and insights. Basically, you should share YOU! Your fans want to know more about you. They want to stay connected to you and see what it is like to be you. So, let them in. You can share things that happen during your day, your perspective during special events, or your thoughts on your business, industry, and life in general. However, there is a caveat. If you are a brand known for one thing, venturing into other areas and giving your perspective on completely different subject matters can cause you to experience some backlash. Nevertheless, as long as you are able to handle it, just be you.

- <u>The Insider</u> – Just like individuals getting personal with their fans, organizations need to give their customers/fans more access to their products, events, business, and everyday happenings. This does not entail telling all of your organizational secrets. Still, the more access you give to your customers and fans, the more they feel like they are part of your organization. Thus, they become more vested in products, services, and your organization's overall successes.

- <u>Numbers Don't Lie</u> – Impactful statistics, educational data or insightful information is a great way to educate your fans and customers and show your expertise in your industry. By providing this type of content, especially infographics, your organization can become a resource of industry information and be considered a key source of data in your area of expertise. The best part about providing factual information is that it is less likely to be disputed as opinion or guesswork. While providing your company's perspective on key industry topics is a great way to develop content, sometimes people want the facts presented in an innovative way.

- <u>Keep the Multimedia Coming</u> – Though it was previously stated, it must be said again: Photos, images, graphics, and videos are the most engaging types of content for Social Media networks. There are entire networks built around photos and videos. So, make sure your brand has multimedia content in addition to text-based content that you can push out to your networks and engage your audience.

Social Media Ads

In May 2012, Facebook's IPO changed the entire Social Media industry. How? Facebook officially went from a social network to a For-Profit Corporation. Their focus went from connecting people to generating revenue, thereby bringing about the next phase in Social Media and social advertising. This evolution took the industry from free platforms that people used to stay connected with their friends to big data advertising platforms that could be used to tell marketers more about us and our online habits than we could ever conceive. The key factor to making Social Media a revenue generator was online advertising. This type of advertising was shown by Google to be quite an effective moneymaking tool. As a result, Twitter, YouTube, SnapChat, and Pinterest all have built-in advertising platforms! As consumers and organizations use Social Media, we are starting to see that our traditional free methods of communicating and posting content, images, videos, and so on may not yield the same results that they used to. Now, the question is, "Must Social Media ads be used in order to be effective on Social Media?"

Organic Reach

When Facebook introduced Edgerank, the formula that determines the information that appears in the newsfeed, it was one of the many steps Facebook took in limiting what is called organic reach. Organic reach is the number of friends and fans we could communicate with on their platform for free. Take, for example, you having 1000 friends/fans on your Facebook page. When you post, an average of only 4% of your audience will see the post. If you want the rest of your friends/fans and others on Facebook to see your post, you have to promote the post using their paid advertising features that we will discuss a little later in the book. Likewise, Facebook limits how much content we see in our newsfeeds. They try to keep it to the most important 100 stories. Mark Zuckerberg stated, "Of the 1,500 stories that could theoretically appear on the average Facebook feed every day, most people only have time to consume roughly 100 stories." Additionally, Facebook most often displays in your newsfeed the stories, articles, videos, and other content you most agree with. The reason for this is the more you agree with the content, the longer you will stay on Facebook. The longer you stay on Facebook, the more ads they can show you. The more ads they show you, the more money they make.

There are ways to increase your organic reach and build an audience for free, but the process takes time, effort, and a consistent flow of content. First, let us look at what Facebook Edgerank uses when it filters what shows up in the newsfeed and who sees what content. One of the most important aspects is the type of content that is posted. If you want to build organic reach, the best options are photos, text, and videos. Additional aspects include how often the user interacts with your profile or page, how long the post has been up, a user's interaction with Facebook ads, and the device and Internet speed of a user. While these are contributing factors to organic reach, Facebook's Edgerank has hundreds of factors they measure to determine what appears in the newsfeed. We discussed earlier the strategies to use to increase social media engagement and connections. Now would be a great time to go back and review those tips and pointers.

Organic reach is not limited to just Facebook. The concept is based on reaching and engaging with people on any Social Media platform without having to pay. Platforms such as Twitter and YouTube have ways to measure organic reach vs. paid reach, and the strategies to reach users on those platforms for free are similar to Facebook with a few differences. Finally, I have to admit something. As I have watched Social Media grow as an industry, I have discovered that the best results on the major platforms (Facebook, Twitter, Google+, LinkedIn, Instagram, YouTube, Pinterest) come from using ads and paid ads.

Pay to Play

Even though our usage of Social Media is free, the platforms that have millions of users are for-profit corporations. Thus, they need to generate a profit. In order to generate this profit, Social Media is following the Google Ads model, where they show these millions of online users ads while they are using the networks. While most organizations that use Social Media want to find the best ways to use it for free, you must to pay-to-play to get the best results. By using the ad platforms and paying to reach larger audiences, you can get exponentially better results in comparison to free, organic usage. Here is the best part: Online advertising can be customized to any budget of any size. Therefore, if your organization has a budget from $100 to $10,000 per month, you can be effective in reaching larger online audiences. Now, we will examine some of the platforms and how to use them to reach audiences.

Social Media Networks to Use

There are numerous Social Media websites, and it would take quite a long time to focus on them individually. So, we will focus only on the major ones. These are the networks you hear about the most and seem to have the most users.

Facebook

This is, by far, the biggest Social Media site today. It has over 1 billion registered users and is growing daily. Each day, there are over 100 million status updates that directly translate to tons of usage. Updates can be text, photos, videos, links, questions, and pretty much whatever a person is doing in the organization. Facebook has two types of pages a user can set up. One is a

Profile page. This is where a user posts information about their day, their life, and their friends. When a user makes a post to their profile page, their friends see what was added and can comment on it. Most recently, profile pages have been updated with the "Subscribe" feature that allows users to post "Public" for all "Subscribed" users to see and comment. Another page a user can setup is a Fan page. A Fan page displays a business, organization, brand, product, artist, band, or cause. Organizations usually have a Fan page. Users of Facebook can become a Fan of the page and receive information and changes when they are posted.

What is the difference between a Facebook Profile page and a Fan page? The bottom line is Profiles are only for individuals, and Fan pages are for organizations and high-profile personal brands. Profiles and Fan pages have different features. Here are some features of Profile pages:

- Profile pages have a limitation of 5,000 friends.
- Profile pages have distinct privacy features and are only accessed if the profile owner "adds you as a friend."
- Profile pages have all the features of Facebook, such as updating statuses, photos, links, videos, applications, groups, wall posts, and other interactive elements.
- Profile pages do not have customizable tabs similar to Fan pages.
- Profile pages are much more common on Facebook and are easily created from the Facebook.com homepage by filling out a few boxes to get started.

On the other hand, Fan pages, also known as Business pages, have these rules and features:

- Businesses are only allowed to open Fan pages, NOT Profile pages. A business that opens a Profile page is in direct violation of the Terms Of Service.

- Business pages allow other users to become Fans, but access by the business to the Fans' individual Profile pages is limited.

- Business pages do not allow the ability to invite friends. In fact, business pages cannot maintain a friends list. They can only maintain a Fan list.

- Business pages allow the updating of status, which gets shared with your Fans. However, Facebook limits the ability to reach the entire Fan page membership. Currently, Facebook only allows Fan pages to reach 10% - 30% of Fan membership.

- Business pages allow pictures, videos, discussion boards, applications, wall posts, groups, and other interactive elements.

- Business pages allow customization of tabs to promote interactivity.

The key to getting people to follow a Facebook user are: (a) post quality content often; (b) make status updates; (c) upload videos and photos; (d) interact with fans to increase engagement; and (e) provide links to other sites and information.

Here, in descending order, are the best types of content to post on Facebook:

1. Photos.
2. Video.
3. Status updates with just text (inspirational quotes, words of wisdom, etc.).
4. Status updates with Links.

5. Events.

Facebook is the leader among Social Media sites. With Facebook, a user can sign into their account and post a status that says they are in a happy mood today, and everyone who is a "Friend" (become members of their particular page) or "subscribed" to them will see the status and can respond back with their own messages, photos, or videos. That's Social Media! It allows for instant interaction between users. It also allows a user to read and react to another user's content. With Social Media, Person A can follow the events of Person B's day in addition to Person B's other friends. With Social Media, information flows fast like a gossip grapevine in a small town.

How can Facebook help your organization? With over 1 billion people on Facebook and a variety ways to send out content, this is one of the best ways to take your content to the people. Since many people are on Facebook, as long as your organization is interacting and keeping the flow of content fresh, people will respond accordingly.

What are EdgeRank and Facebook NewsFeed Optimization?
Facebook uses the EdgeRank algorithm to determine what is displayed in our News Feeds. The official definition of EdgeRank is, "an algorithm developed by Facebook to govern what is displayed—and how high—on the News Feed." Edgerank consists of Affinity, Weight, and Decay. Affinity is the score between the viewing user and the creator. Basically it is how close a relationship you have with the brand or person pushing out the content, and how often you like,

share, comment, or even click on their posts. Weight is based on how you communicate with the brand or person. Do you comment, like, or share more? Each type of interaction has a weight associated with it. Finally, Decay refers to Time Decay and how long it has been since you interacted with that person or brand. The older the contact, the less valuable the relationship and the less likely Facebook will allow their content to appear in your News Feed.

Edgerank is what goes into Facebook News Feed Optimization. Brands have to be conscious of what content they push out because they want to increase engagement and their Edgerank score with their followers. If, on average, only 16% of your fans/friends see your posts, the only way to increase your score is to create content that people interact with more, thus creating a deeper online relationship with you and your brand.

The reason for these changes is based on one premise: "Facebook is a business first, then a network." They have to monetize their network. The best way to do that is to advertise to us based on our likes and updates and make us pay to reach our entire audience online, which is why they introduced promoted posts.

Promoted Posts and Ads

Facebook ads and Promoted Posts are great ways to find the right customers for your business. You can design your creative ad including the headline, body text, and images. This will help you connect with people who have not, until now, connected to your Facebook business page.

Interestingly, people may like your page after they click your ad. This means more chances of it appearing in their newsfeed. This can very well translate into more business and profits over time, and you surely want this to happen. Ads appear on the right side of the Facebook page and give people an interactive way to be drawn in and connect with your fan page. Promoted Posts are posts that you put onto your Fan page and pay to have promoted (placed into the newsfeeds) of your Fans and their Friends. Facebook gives you a range of people that will see your promoted post, based on the amount you pay and the number of Fans on your page. For example, if you have 400 Facebook Fans, you may pay $15 to promote your post to 4000 people. Likewise, if you have one million Fans, you could end up paying $4000 to reach another million people.

How to setup Facebook Profile account

1. Go to http://www.Facebook.com and look for the boxes underneath the text that says, "Sign Up – It's free and always will be." Input your First Name, Last Name, Email, Email again, Password, Gender, and Birthday. Once you have completed that, click the green "Sign Up" button.

2. Click "Skip" on "Step 1, Find Friends," unless you want to search your contact lists for the email providers and services listed. "Step 2 – Profile Information." Add your Profile information, such as High School, College, and Employer. When you are done, click the blue "Save & Continue" button.

3. Step 3 – "Profile Picture" is where you add a picture of yourself. You can upload the photo from your computer or take a photo with your webcam. When you are done, click the blue "Save & Continue" button.

4. Start using your new Facebook page. Once you have uploaded your picture and searched for people you may know, you can click the "News Feed" button on the left and post your first status.

How to Create a Facebook Fan Page

1. Go to www.Facebook.com/pages and select the category your organization falls under. The top choices are usually "Local Business or Place" or "Cause or Community."

2. Choose a category that your organization falls under from the dropdown menu. Next, type in the name of your organization and the following lines asking for the address and phone number. Finally, check the box that says "I agree to Facebook Pages Terms" and click on "Get Started."

3. Now that you have created your Fan page, start customizing it so that you can use it. Let's focus on the basics. Upload an image so that people can associate your Fan page with some type of image. Your logo is a great choice here.

4. Next, provide some basic information about your organization and a link to your website. Once you are done, click "Save Info."

5. Now, let's move on to setting up your new Facebook Timeline Fan Page. First, make sure to like your new Fan page. You are not only creating the page. You are the first Fan. Congrats!

6. Next, invite your friends, import contacts from your organization mailing list, and start notifying people that this new Fan page is available.

7. Post your first status, letting people know that this page is live!

8. Make sure to continue customizing your new page, and do not forget to upload your cover image!

Facebook Fan Pages have 5 tabs at the top that are key to the way they function and their administration.

- Page - Actual Facebook Fan Page.
- Activity – Page Recent Notifications and Posts, Scheduled Posts, and Drafts.
- Insights - Facebook analytics information.
- Settings - Page settings and account information, such as Page Visibility, Posting Ability, Page info, Notifications, Page Roles, Mobile, Page Moderation, and much more.
- Help - Visit Help Center, Send Feedback, and Facebook Help Community.

How to Setup a Facebook Ad

Facebook is one of the most widely used Social Media websites. Because of this, Facebook ads are a great way to find the right customers for your business. You can design your creative ad, including the headline, body text, and images. This will help you connect with people who have not connected to your Facebook Business page, until now.

Interestingly, people may like your page after they click your ad, and this means more chances of appearing in their newsfeed. This can very well translate into more business and profits over time. As stated before, you surely want this to happen.

One of the easiest forms of Facebook Ads is the "Boost Post" option that we see on Fan Pages. This button appears at the lower right of a post and gives you the option to make your post more visible. Once you click that button, you get an option to target your audience based on interests, demographics, and other relevant factors. Once you have chosen your audience, you can choose the amount you want to pay. Keep in mind that the more you pay, the larger the audience that will see your post. When users see your post, they will see "Sponsored" on the post letting them know that you paid for this ad. The best part about the "Boost Post" feature is the analytics that come with it. These let you know how many people saw your post, engaged with the post, shared the post, and commented.

Here is how you can launch your ad campaign on Facebook and reach a larger number of target customers. Login to your Facebook account and look at the top right corner of your screen. Click the tiny arrow icon and look in the dropdown for the "Create Ads or Manage Ads" option. Another option is to go to http://facebook.com/ads. You can read up on how to setup a Facebook Ad, or you can click on the "Manage Your Ads" button and get started.

The Facebook Ads Dashboard has many options that include the following:

- Campaigns - This tab shows your current campaigns, as well as new campaigns that you may want to start.
- Pages - This tab contains the Facebook Fan pages you manage along with different ads, boosts, and features they have.

61

- Reports - This tab gives you detailed reports on the success or failure of your campaigns and what you can do to make them better.

- Audience Insights - This is the Facebook Analytics feature that analyzes the people on Facebook and gives you the ability to create audiences for whom you can target your campaigns.

- Settings - This tab contains your account information, name of organization, and address.

- Billing - The billing tab is where you input your financial information (credit card, paypal, etc.) and see charges for your ads.

- Conversion Tracking - This tab creates a tracking pixel that you can add to your website. The pixel is a small piece of code that will send information about the success of your ads back to Facebook.

- Power Editor - This is an advanced editor for Facebook Campaigns and ads. In addition to creating advanced campaigns and ads, you can download data from this tab for analysis and other uses.

- Account History - This is a history of different things you have done within your Facebook Ads account for you to recall, duplicate, or analyze.

- Audiences - This section is where you can create custom-targeted audiences for your Facebook Campaigns. These audiences can be similar to the audience that comes to your website ("look alike" audience), as well as an audience you customize with Facebook targeted features.

- Help Center - This is the Facebook-created section designed for marketers, business owners, and other individuals looking to professionally promote their brand on Facebook.

- Advertiser Support – This is a Community Support area that provides solutions, success stories, and news on how to use Facebook Pages and the Ad center. You can join the Help Community and get help from other users.

Once you click "Create a Campaign," you will arrive at the "Campaign Objectives" page.

- Boost Your Posts - Get more people to see and engage with your Page posts.
- Promote Your Page - Connect more people with your Page.
- Send People to Your Website - Increase the number of visits to your website.
- Increase Conversions on Your Website - Send people to your website to take a specific action, like signing up for a newsletter. Remember to use a conversion pixel to measure your results.
- Get Installs of Your App - Send people to the store where they can purchase your app.
- Increase Engagement in Your App - Get more people to use your Facebook or mobile app.
- Reach People Near Your Business - Promote your business to people nearby.
- Raise Attendance at Your Event - Promote your Facebook Page's event to increase your attendance.
- Get People to Claim Your Offer - Promote timely discounts and other deals for people to claim in your store.
- Get Video Views - Promote videos that show behind-the-scenes footage, product launches, or customer stories to raise awareness about your brand.

- <u>Help Choosing an Objective</u> - Click here to let Facebook help you decide what you want to achieve with your Facebook ads and assist you in creating ads that will get results.

Overall, as we look at the numerous options Facebook Ads offer—there being so many more than we can explain in this one book—we see that Facebook has a great platform to reach millions of people with great built-in advertising software. As Facebook continues to become more "Pay to Play" and organic reach decreases, Facebook Ads will continue to become an important part of Social Media strategies.

<u>Facebook Insights</u>

Facebook Insights provides information about your page's performance and are available after 30 people like your page. Find demographic data about your audience and see how people are discovering and responding to your posts. Insights is an extensive section on Facebook Fan pages that analyzes their Social Media posts and gives information on how impactful they are. The Insights tab is located at the top of your Facebook Fan page. This is where you find all your Facebook Analytics information.

To the far right, the "Export" and "Promote Business" options are useful. There are six key tabs on the Insights tab. They are:

- <u>Overview</u> - In the Overview section of your Insights, you will find the following information about your page's overall performance:

- o *Page Likes*: Total page Likes is number of unique people who like your page. "New page Likes" shows the number of new Likes your page received during the last 7 days in comparison to the previous 7-day period.

- o *Post Reach*: Total Reach is the number of unique people who have seen any content associated with your page, including ads during the last 7 days. Post Reach shows the number of unique people who have seen your page posts.

- o *Engagement*: People Engaged is the number of unique people who have clicked, Liked, commented on or shared your posts during the last 7 days. Likes, Comments, Shares and Post Clicks show the totals for these actions during the last 7 days.

- <u>Likes</u> - Shows the number of times your page was Liked during a specific date range.

- <u>Reach</u> - You can see how many people are Liking, commenting on, and sharing your page posts.

  - o *Gender and age*: The percentage of people who saw any content about your page for each age and gender bracket, based on the info people entered in their personal profiles.

  - o *Countries*: The number of people who saw any content about your page grouped by country and based on IP address.

  - o *Cities*: The number of people who saw any content about your page grouped by city and based on IP address.

  - o *Language*: The number of people who saw any content about your page grouped by language and based on default language settings.

- <u>Visits</u> - Shows the number of times that each of your page tabs (ex: Timeline, Info Tab) was viewed.
    - o You can see the external sources that are referring traffic to your page during a specific date range.
- <u>Posts</u> - Learn which posts have the most Likes, reach, and engagement.
- <u>People</u> - Shows data of when your audience is on Facebook and their demographic information.
    - o The percentage of people who Like your page for each age and gender bracket, based on the data people entered on their personal profiles.
    - o The countries and cities of the people who Like your Page, based on their IP address and when they use Facebook.
    - o The language of the people who Like your Page, based on their default language settings.

Twitter

Twitter is a service that allows a user to send out very short messages of 140 characters or less. It works on a similar principle as Facebook in that a user sets up an account and people can follow it. Twitter is much like standing on a hill and shouting out a message to the village below. As long as someone has selected the message-giver's account to follow, they will receive the message. On Twitter, you can gain a large number of followers quickly because the messages are so short that recipients do not mind receiving them. With +500 million users and +100 million tweets a day, the audience is ready to listen and interact.

How can Twitter help your organization?

You need to get people to follow your Twitter account. The key is to tweet often with great content, participate in conversations with other users, and share great content. You can also take other users' tweets and retweet them. You can even tweet links to content you like, as well as send multimedia and photos. Following other users may bring you more followers when the users decide to reciprocate and follow you. Interact and let them know that you will be there when they reach out to you via Twitter.

Make sure to use the hashtag (#) for your company's benefit and control the conversation. The hashtag on Twitter is how people categorize the tweets they send out. Gary Vee said, "Twitter is the best Social Media platform because it allows anyone to jump into any conversation using a hashtag to speak, learn, and participate with a community around that topic." Twitter chats are a great example of communities that are built around a hashtag. Moderators will ask questions on Twitter using the community hashtag, and people monitor the hashtag for questions and responses and use the hashtag to communicate. These communities provide great opportunities to find key people to follow, allow people to follow you, and establish your organization as a key resource in the community.

How to setup a Twitter account

1. Go to http://www.Twitter.com, and sign up for an account under the "New to Twitter?" box. Enter your full name, email address, and password, and click the yellow "Sign Up" button.

2. You will go to a page that has the information you just inserted. Choose a username, and click the yellow "Create My Account" button.

3. Unless you want to search your contact lists for the email providers and services listed, skip "Suggestions", "Interests," and "Friends." Once you finally get to your Twitter page as shown below, go to the top right and click on your username. Then, go to the "Settings" tab.

Click on the "Profile" link, and add a profile picture. If you want to, you may change your name, update the location of your organization, enter your website, and insert a small bio about your organization so people can know this is the official Twitter page. Finally, click the blue "Save" button and your page will be updated. Click the "Home" option on the black bar at the top of the page and you will get back to your Twitter homepage. Now, you can start tweeting.

Enhance Your Profile Page

Remember that you can actually boost your business when you have an impressive profile page. You can pick your business name as your username. Make sure you upload an image that becomes the "face" of your business. Insert your location and website, and it is always good to write a brief bio describing what your business does. Be sure to add a great profile picture, a high-quality cover photo, and choose a memorable username.

Twitter Ads and Sponsored Tweets

Twitter ads and Sponsored Tweets are a great way to find the right customers for your business. You can allow your account to be featured on Twitter and get people to "follow" you, or you can take tweets that you have sent out and "promote" them so they appear in people's timelines. The more timelines you appear in, the more likely people are to follow your Twitter account. Twitter has just recently allowed businesses and personal accounts to create and run ads. You can create and access Twitter ads at Ads.Twitter.com.

Setting up Twitter Advertising

You can create your own Twitter ads and boost your business awareness on one of the most popular social network websites. For this, you have to sign in to your Twitter account. Then, go to http://ads.twitter.com.

Twitter ads continue to become a very powerful platform for reaching the hundreds of millions of Twitter users. With the ability to customize your ad campaign based on a variety of platforms, locations, outcomes, demographics, and more, Twitter ads are a great way to use online ad budgets and receive a great ROI (return on investment).

Step 1. Setup your funding source. Choose which credit card you want to add to your account. If you are just testing out Twitter ads to see how well it can work for you, use a pre-paid credit card with a preset limit to see how well your campaign does without being overcharged.

Step 2. Create a New Campaign. Click the "Create New Campaign" button and choose which type of campaign you want based on the results you are trying to achieve.

- Followers - This is the best option to gain more followers on your Twitter account and increase your online audience.
- Website Clicks or Conversions - This is the go-to option for getting users to click on a link for a sale or Twitter card and visiting your website and completing a sale or signup form.
- Tweet Engagements - If you want engagement on your tweet, try using this option. Engagement can include responses, retweets, and Favorites (Likes).
- App Installs or Engagements – Try this option if you want users to install your app and interact with the app and/or tweet.
- Leads on Twitter – Choose this option if you are looking for high-quality leads on Twitter. If you are trying to find key users based on certain key attributes, this information will help maximize your campaign.

- <u>Custom</u> - This is the best option if you want to customize and get a variety of results from your campaign.

- <u>Help Me Choose</u> - If you cannot figure out which campaign is best for you, choose this option and let Twitter Ads help you choose your campaign.

Once you have chosen your campaign option, you can optimize your campaign even further with location, devices, platforms, and other key demographic information. You can use this information to seek out and target an audience. This will help give your campaign the best results.

<u>Twitter Analytics</u>

Twitter Analytics is a great way to measure engagement, increase followers, and use premium Twitter features to grow your online Twitter audience. In order to get Twitter Analytics, you need to become an advertiser and setup a payment option for online campaigns. When you have setup your Twitter ads account, you will be able to start monitoring and measuring your current Twitter efforts all while seeing how you can better reach your audience.

- <u>Tweet activity</u> - Measure engagement and learn how to make your Regular and Promoted Tweets more successful. Twitter activity, such as Impressions and Engagement Rate, are key factors that are measured.

- Followers - Explore the interests, locations, demographics, and other key Twitter users that your followers follow. This tab also shows the growth of your account over the last 24 months.

- Twitter Cards - Track how your Twitter Cards drive clicks, app installs, and Retweets. Twitter cards are interactive Tweets where you see buttons, videos playing, and other programmed features paid for in Twitter.

Overall, Twitter Analytics gives you a great overview of your Twitter account and how your Tweets are doing with your audience. This is a marvelous way to measure your Social Media strategy and see whether or not it is productive. Here are some key tips on how to take the information provided by Twitter Analytics and develop a better strategy. Once you gather your Twitter Activity for a set timeframe (last 365 days), you can export that information from Twitter in Excel/CSV format. Once you have this data in the desired format, you can open it up and sort it by key factors. With it, you will see which Tweet had the most engagement, most retweets, most replies, and so on. As you gather this information, you will discover the topics, tweets, and wording that resonates with your audience and yields the best results.

Google+

Google+ is the newest social network and has rapidly increased its user base. Its functionality is similar to Facebook, but with a few differences. One of the best things I have noticed about Google+ is the tremendous potential it has for integration with other Google apps and services.

It is impossible to believe that Google+ was not thinking "mobile" from day one. This long-term vision will help Google+ last far into the future. The biggest benefit of Google+ is its heavy integration into Google Search. Google Search indexes Google+, and things that are located within that network come up higher in search results. To increase its online visibility, it is imperative your organization has a presence on this network.

- <u>Business Profiles</u> - Business profiles are one of the best features of Google+. They are very similar to Facebook Fan pages in terms of setup and functionality. You can create a Google+ Business page from your Google+ account, manage it yourself, or add other Google+ users to manage it for you. Managers can post on the page, moderate comments, upload photos, and maintain the page.

- <u>Circles</u> - Basically, this lets you organize the people you know into groups so you can communicate only with them. Friends, parents, co-workers, and/or acquaintances can all be placed in different circles.

- <u>Hangouts</u> - Group video chat anyone? If multiple friends are online, you can all get together face-to-face! You can even watch YouTube videos with one another. Small groups can meet online via video chat and interact with each other. If they decide not to use video chat, the Messenger is a handy option. Messenger is simply a group chat without the video. You can also record the videos with the "Hangout on Air" feature.

This allows Google+ users to broadcast Hangouts live and record them to a YouTube channel. Imagine a webinar where up to 10 people were interacting live with the CEO and up to 1,000 were watching the broadcast. These are the types of possibilities Google Hangouts possesses.

- Communities - This is the newest feature of Google+ and the second best feature of the network. Communities are similar to Facebook groups, but with many more functions and better controls. Google Communities allow users to build small communities within Google+ around topics, brands, or anything they find interesting. From there, they can communicate on those topics and stay informed.

With all these features, I believe Google+ has some great opportunities to make an impact online, and you should really consider it.

How to Setup a Google+ Account

Log on to https://plus.google.com/. If you already have a Gmail/Google account, just provide the email and password and click the "Sign In" button. However, at this point, I will assume you do not have an account on Google. Click on the red "Sign Up" Button and provide your name, user name, password, gender, date of birth, mobile phone, location, etc. At the bottom of the page, do not forget to check the box next to "I agree to the Google Terms of Service and Privacy Policy."

<u>Set Up Your Profile</u>

When all is done, click on the blue "Next Step" button at the bottom of the page. Here, you will be asked to provide a profile photo. You can upload your picture and set it as your profile photo using the "Add Profile Photo" button. You can choose to skip this step and click the "Next" button.

Click on the blue "Continue to Google+" button, and you will see the following options: (1) Click on the "Add People" tab. You will be able to follow pages and people from all walks of life, such as Causes, Sports, Lifestyle, and more; (2) Click on the second tab that is "Be Awesome," and you can fill out more profile information.

From there, you are asked to upload your photo. If your webcam is detected, you can instantly snap one. Moreover, you can provide additional information about yourself like your profession, education, or residence. As you move ahead, you will find yourself at the Google+ Home Page.

Look at the strip on the extreme left of the page. Here, you will be able to see different options such as Games, Circles, Events, Profile, and more. It is on this strip you will find the option for "Pages." However, if you cannot find it, click on "More" as highlighted above, and you will come to the following symbol for pages. By clicking on the "Pages" icon, all the pages you have previously created will be displayed in the grid highlighted above. You can click on any of these pages to go directly to them. Or, if you want to create a new page, click on the red "Create New Page" button.

Here, you pick a category to which your page will belong. Since we are creating a Business page, we will select "Company, Institution, or Organization." Once you choose this option, further categorize your page by choosing a category from the drop-down box. Afterward, click the blue "Next" button.

Now, you must provide additional information about your Business page, such as the page's name and URL. Furthermore, you have to specify whether your Business page's content is appropriate for everyone or a particular group of people. After checking the box for "Pages Terms," click on the "Continue" button.

This is the final step. Add a cover photo and logo for your page. You will also be asked to describe your page in 10 words and provide a URL so people can contact you. After all this information is provided, just click on the blue "Finish" button at the extreme right and bottom of the page. Congratulations! Your Google+ Business page has been created!

How to Setup a Google Hangout on Air

This is how a typical Google+ stream looks with the Hangouts option on the left. Click on the "Hangouts" icon to get started. Those using Hangouts for the first time can access detailed information by clicking on the "What's a Hangout?" button. In addition to the basic definition, users will be educated as to how they can use this feature to their advantage.

Google+ Hangouts feature YouTube and Google Effects to offer users convenience. Both these apps can be launched directly by clicking the "Launch" button positioned next to the apps' names. The variety of settings for Hangouts can be changed using the "Settings" button. Click on the "Start a Hangout" button. If you do not have the plugin installed, you may be prompted to install the "Hangout Voice Chat Plugin." Select the blue "Install Plugin" button. Below the button is a list of the operating systems providing support for this plugin, such as Windows XP+, Mac OSX 10.5+, and Linux. From here, the user can choose "Run" to download it, or "Cancel" to stop the download.

Start Using Hangout

Once the plugin downloads successfully, users have to provide the requested details to start a Hangout. Users will be required to specify a name for the Hangout as well as the names, email addresses, or circles with which they want to hang out.

Enable or Disable Hangouts on Air

The most crucial part of the entire Hangout experience is to determine if you want yours to be broadcasted to the public or kept private. If you have a message you want a global audience to hear, just check the box next to the "Enable Hangouts on Air" option.

Inviting People to Your Hangout

In case none of the individuals you selected to start a Hangout with are online, the following screen will be displayed.

However, you have no reason to be sad! With the "Invite More" button, you can add new people to a Hangout, or begin a Hangout with those online.

Explore the Options

Apart from inviting people, there are a variety of options of which a user can make use. For instance, users can do the following:

- Chat
- Share screen
- Use Google Effects
- Use Google Drive
- View and use other apps supported by Hangouts on air

Follow the steps listed above to start enjoying Hangouts like never before.

Google Analytics for Social Media

Another great tool that helps in managing analytics is Google Analytics for Social Media. To reach these metrics you need to have a Google account (usually a Gmail account), and you login at http://www.google.com/analytics. Once there, simply look under "Traffic Sources" for the "Social" segment, which can give you an overview of the referrals you receive from each social network, the pages viewed by those visitors, and even the "flow" of each visitor through your site from page to page until they left.

Once you have clicked the "Overview" link to get started, the first thing you will see is an "educational message" from Google Analytics that speaks about the benefits of The Social Relationship and tracking it online.

Another key metric is the social value of a customer, based on how they were referred to your website from a Social Media property. Did they see a direct link from you, or were they referred from a friend who saw a link? This is the difference between a conversion and an assisted social conversion. Here, you will also see which social networks gave you the most traffic.

Make sure you look at the daily referrals from social networks in comparison to the number of overall visitors. This is a great way to measure your Social Media effectiveness against your organic reach. An example report you could develop from Google Analytics would tell you with 100 visitors coming to your site daily, 30% is from Social Media, 30% is from Google ads, and 40% is from direct searches.

YouTube

YouTube.com is the #1 site for video on the entire Internet. It is the second largest search engine behind Google.com. YouTube is also owned by Google Inc. YouTube has over 600 million registered users, more than 10 hours of video uploaded every minute, and it receives two billion views per day. It also has a 20-minute limit for most accounts (some accounts do not have the 20 minute limit) and is mobile device compatible (HTML5).

The question with these amazing stats is, how can uploading videos help your organization? First and foremost, there are millions of viewers on YouTube.com everyday. You can tap into this audience by setting up your video page on YouTube.com. Of course, make sure you only put out content you want the world to see and that reflects the organization in a positive light. You may not have a video that goes viral every time you post something, but the impact of each video is worthwhile. Also, YouTube.com is free! This creates an amazing opportunity to get the visibility and word out about your organization and attract new supporters on and offline. You can let people comment on your videos and subscribe to your video page. You can also become online friends with them so that you can communicate and discuss your videos with your online audience. Finally, with every video uploaded to YouTube, you can get the code from them and embed these videos in your website, thereby creating a multimedia presence. Great videos to put on YouTube are the same videos that we discussed about posting on Facebook: weekly updates, product commercials, and other videos that will help promote and advance your organization online.

How to Upload a Video to YouTube

Go to YouTube.com and "Sign In" (or "Create Account" if you do not have one already) to your account at the top right of the page. Once you are signed in, click "Upload" at the top of the page. Once you click "Upload," you will see the actual "Upload Video Files" page. Now, click the "Select Files from Your Computer" button beneath the large red arrow.

After you click the "Select Files from Your Computer" button, a window will popup that will let you choose the file you want to upload from your desktop. Once you choose the file, the upload process will begin, and you will be able to watch the progress, fill in the video information, and set the privacy settings.

On the "Advanced Settings" tab, you can allow comments and video responses and choose from a host of other options for your videos. After you choose the ones you want, you can either click the blue "Save Changes" button, or you can let YouTube take care of saving it for you since it does this automatically. Once the video is completely uploaded, you can go to the video page by clicking on the "Video Manager" button. From there, you click on the video you want to embed and/or retrieve the link. Then, you can click on the "Share" button beneath the video for the YouTube URL, or you click on the "Embed" button that appears next to the YouTube URL/Link and get the code to place the YouTube video on a website. Once you have the Embed code, you will need someone with some technical expertise, because the embed code is what you want to copy and paste onto your website page.

YouTube's new Creator Studio is the name for all of the features each YouTube channel has. The features include:

- Dashboard - Dashboard is the overview of the YouTube channel with key channel stats and tips to grow your channel. This page is customizable by adding key widgets that show what you would like to see on your YouTube Dashboard page. To add a new widget, click the "Add Widget" option in the upper right (right after views and subscribers) and choose what widget you would like to add from the dropdown menu. The options are "Videos," "Comments," "Key Stats," "What's New?" and "Notifications." If you want to move them around or delete them after adding them to your dashboard, you can do so by mousing over the top right corner of the widget, and you will see the options to move or delete.

- Video Manager - This tab is your Video library where you edit videos, create and populate playlists, enable live streaming, and more. This is one of the most important tabs inside the YouTube Channel.

- Community - This is your social network management tab. Here, you can manage comments on your pages, messages sent to your channel, subscribers, top fans, and much more.

- Channel - This tab has the features of your channel and lets you know the status (good standing) of your channel. Once here, you are able to see if your channel is Partner Verified, if you have any copyright strikes, longer video privileges, monetization features, custom thumbnails, external annotations links, paid subscriptions, and tons more.

- Analytics - This tab has a wealth of analytics information such as engagement, total views, total minutes watched, shares, comments, likes, dislikes, subscribers, earnings, ad performance, demographics, devices watched from, and others.

- Create - This tab provides audio and video editing features. You can add royalty-free music for your project and edit your videos inside of Youtube.

Now that we have gone through an overview of the Creator Studio, I want to point out four key features that every organization should use when building their YouTube channel.

- YouTube Scheduling Feature - When you were previously uploading your videos, you could choose to make the video public, unlisted, or private. Now, there is the "Schedule" option that gives you the choice to specify which date your video will go live. This scheduling feature is a great addition seeing that it continues to add automated features to the amazing YouTube platform.

- YouTube Annotation Feature - In order to get the most out of the YouTube platform, you have to make the user's experience as easy as possible. One of the best ways to do this is to use the "Annotations" feature. Annotations are those popups that show up while you are watching a YouTube video. You click these popups and something happens. The options available are giving users the choices to subscribe from within the video, open a new video, go to an external website, and more. Do not allow users to watch your videos and simply go away. Give them options to subscribe to your social networks and visit your website so you may gather their information and keep in touch with them.

  Great examples of this include giving viewers a link to purchase a show or message while they are watching it. When users are close to the end of watching a video, give them the option to subscribe to your YouTube channel. Additionally, if you want to gather more information from your viewers, offer them a free download while they are watching your videos, and give them a link to your website to give their information and subscribe.

- YouTube Playlists Feature - When users come to your YouTube channel, do not make your videos hard to sort. Create playlists people can easily navigate. When you are on Netflix, you can watch an entire season from that page's main screen. Likewise, when you have a series of videos that have a common theme, place them in a playlist so users can watch all of them from the same screen. As you upload more videos, you will discover that disorganization comes along with the territory. This leads to users losing interest in searching your channel. Let your playlists guide users through your YouTube channel and keep them engaged.

- <u>YouTube Descriptions and Keywords</u> - Descriptions and keywords are key to the relevance of your YouTube channel. YouTube is the second largest search engine in the world, and the way videos are indexed is via keywords and descriptions. The more you add accurate descriptions and keywords to your videos, the easier they are to find.

<u>YouTube Ads</u>

Deliver your message to the right people at the right time with video ads. Every business has an audience on YouTube. YouTube ads are tied into the Google AdWords platform. When you set up an AdWords account, you can associate it with your YouTube account. From there, the results for all your advertising efforts can be measured.

<u>Getting Started</u>

Go to http://YouTube.com/ads and click on the "Get Started" button on the top right of the page. There are three steps to launching a YouTube ad. They are:

- Step 1: Upload your video to YouTube - This will be your ad.

- Step 2: Create an AdWords account - YouTube video ads are powered by Google AdWords (google.com/adwords). After you create an account, this is where you will manage your ads and check results.

- Step 3: Launch your video ad – Here, you will select your video, decide who will see it, where it will show up, and how much you desire to spend.

If you already have a YouTube account with a video that you want to use as an ad, you can use the following process:

Go to http://YouTube.com/ads and click on the "Start Advertising on YouTube" button.

- Step 1. Select Your Video from your list of current videos.

- Step 2. Create Your Video Ad - Choose your Ad headline, Ad Description, and a video thumbnail for the ad. Decide where you want to send users who click your ad (YouTube channel or your website).

- Step 3. Choose how much you want to spend for this ad.

- Step 4. Choose your audience (if you want to target a specific audience with certain characteristics).

- Step 5. Click the "Skip Campaign Creation" or "Save and Continue" options to create your Google AdWords account.

- Step 6. Set up your billing options.

- Step 7. Review and launch your ad

YouTube Analytics

YouTube Analytics provides insights, data, and metrics to help you regularly assess your channel's performance and investigate changes or trends across key metrics. YouTube Analytics also gives actionable insights for organizations to make better videos, develop strategic programming, and implement and measure optimizations. YouTube Analytics helps you figure out who your viewers are, what they want to watch, how they are watching, how long they are watching, from where they are watching, and what makes them come and go. This is no surprise as YouTube is owned by Google, and their analytics software is second to none.

How to Use YouTube Analytics

Login to YouTube. Next, click on the profile pic at the top right to see the dropdown menu. Once you have that, click on the "Creator Studio" option. This will take you to your YouTube dashboard. From here, click the "Analytics" tab in the menu, and you will arrive at the "Overview" page. There are numerous Analytics options in this menu to help you get an abundance of information on your audience. Analytics options include:

- Overview - Gives you an overview of your entire channel analytics. This glimpse gives you a 28-day look at your top videos, engagement, Views, Shares, Comments, Subscribers, and more.
- Real-time - This is real-time statistics for your channel. This gives you an overview of what is currently happening on your channel and what has happened over the last 48 hours.

- Estimated Earnings/Ad Performance - If you have AdSense associated with your YouTube account and active Ads, this is where you will see how much you have earned.

- Views - This tab shows how many views your channel received over the specified timeframe and how many views each individual video received. Also, you can see how many views were received from each country and on which dates these views occurred.

- Demographics - This tab shows the demographics of your channel based on country, age, and gender.

- Playback Locations - This tab shows playback locations (where users watched your videos) such as the YouTube Channel, other websites, external apps, etc.

- Traffic Sources - This tab shows how people found your YouTube videos. Did they see it as a suggested video somewhere? Did they search for it on Google? Did your website refer them? Did they watch it in a series on a playlist, or did a YouTube ad bring them there?

- Devices - This tab shows the devices people are using to watch your videos, be they mobile phones, computers, tablets, televisions, game consoles, internet television consoles, and more.

- Audience Retention - This tab shows how long people, on average, are watching your channel's videos. It also shows how long people are watching each video.

- Subscribers - This tab shows how many subscribers your channel gained and lost. It also lets you know from where they subscribed, whether it was via the channel, from a video, from a recommendation, or elsewhere.

- Likes and Dislikes - This tab shows how many Likes and Dislikes your channel received. It also shows which videos received Likes/Dislikes and how many.

- Favorites - This tab shows how many Favorites your channel received. It also shows which videos received Favorites and how many.

- Comments - This tab shows how many Comments your channel received. It also shows which videos received Comments and how many.

- Sharing - This tab shows how many Shares your channel has received. It also shows which videos were Shared and how many times.

- Annotations - This tab shows which Annotations on which videos were successful in being clicked, which ones were closed, and what percentage of clicks and closes each video received.

Overall, this information is invaluable for organizations looking to establish a significant YouTube presence. It showcases the benefits of a YouTube channel while highlighting the drawbacks of irrelevant video content.

Instagram

One billion dollars! That is the first thought that comes to my mind when I think about Instagram. When Facebook paid that amount for them, they were just a niche social network that a few million people used to share photos. Now, they are a 200 million-member, mobile Social Media network that has become the #1 destination to share photos on mobile devices, and the number of users is growing. Along with their heavy integration into Facebook, they have established themselves as a great example of a mobile network driven by visual content. When you share a photo or video in Instagram, you can also choose to share it with Facebook and Twitter. Organizations have a great opportunity to share images of their content via this network and build an online audience here. There are many opportunities to share products and services, and using pictures with this visual Social Media network is a great way to see your business in action. All a company needs is a smartphone and an organization's connection, and they can start sharing photos of great things.

Instagram is much more than just a photo and video-sharing app. It has implemented some great new features that have taken this platform to a whole new level. Hyperlapse, an Instagram created app, is a new app used to capture high-quality time lapse videos, even while in motion, and share these videos on Instagram. Instagram also has updated editing features that allow comments and caption editing. Finally, instead of being satisfied with what they already created, they added additional video and photo filters. Now, when you go to select a filter, you will see a new wrench icon. Tap it, and you will find a tray of photo editing tools ready for you to explore. Now, you can also adjust how much of a filter you apply to a photo by double tapping the filter icon.

Instagram Key Statistics
- +300 Million users
- 20 Billion photos shared
- 1.6 Billion likes daily
- 60 Million photos per day

How to setup an Instagram account

Here is how you can create an account on Instagram and take advantage of this exciting, free app for iOS and Android. First, go to http://instagram.com/ and download the Instagram app for iPhone, iPod, and iPad from the iTunes App Store, or Google Play for Android devices.

Once the download is complete, click the app and start the registration process. Once the app is open, click "Register," and you will be guided to a new screen. Tap "Use Your Facebook Info" and enter your account details. Your Facebook username will be displayed, and this is how people can find you. You can also use the name of your business to promote your business. Once you finish entering the details, tap "Register." You will be given an option to invite your Facebook friends. Tap "Skip" if you do not want to invite people. Instagram will also ask you to check which of your phone contacts use the same app. If you are not interested in knowing more, click "Skip."

Now, your Instagram account is created, and you can set up an amazing profile. Look at the bottom of your screen, and you will find 5 different icons. Press the rectangle icon at the far right corner to see profile settings. You can enter your website, first and last name, profile photo, and a short bio, too. Once you have finished editing your profile, hit "Save." If there is anything interesting you want to capture or share with your friends, click the camera icon in the center.

Pick the source (i.e. select "Camera") and choose if you want to snap a photo or record a video. Additionally, you can choose "Photo Gallery" to upload an image or video from your phone. You can apply different filters to your photo or video from the choices that appear on the screen. Click "Next" once you have finished making the changes.

Type a caption to tell something about your photo, then click the social network on which you want to share your photo. Even if your account is not linked, you can enter your username and password to associate it with Instagram. Click "Done" to post your photo on your favorite Social Media website.

Instagram Ads

Instagram recently launched their ads feature. Ads appear in users' newsfeeds with a "Sponsored" tag on them similar to Facebook Ads. Instagram is taking the same approach to ads that other major social networks have taken by initially allowing them to be available to major corporate partners before other organizations can use the feature. Instagram ads is a great feature to consider for your Social Media strategy because the network has a very engaged following and is one of the few networks that appeal to older and younger generations. Instagram's aim is to make any advertisements you see feel as natural to Instagram as the photos and videos many of you already enjoy from your favorite brands. Other key features that could be gathered in Instagram ads are location, demographics, phone type, data usage, and other relevant information.

Pinterest

Pinterest is the new kid on the block, its focus being on photos and the sharing ("pinning") of them in a poster board format. With this network, organizations can create inspirational and informational photos that can be posted to boards that are based around certain themes for which people can search. For example, if your organization creates a board on Products, they can post photos of people using your products and let other pinners repin those photos. You can also post links to videos on Pinterest, which is a largely unknown feature. Thus, in addition to product photos, you can post actual videos of people using your products.

Pinterest Key Statistics

- 70 Million Users
- 80% of Pinterest users are female.
- 158 pins is the average number that each female user has posted.

How to setup a Pinterest account:

Visit http://pinterest.com/ and click the red button that says "Join Pinterest." You will see 3 choices to sign up to Pinterest. You can connect it with your Facebook or Twitter account. The biggest advantage of using your Twitter or Facebook login details is that you can easily connect with your friends. If neither of these choices do not appeal to you, simply click "Sign up with your Email Address." However, you will have to build your Friends list from scratch.

Once you provide your email address or account information, you will be guided to a screen where you can create your Pinterest account. Choose a unique username for your Pinterest account. If you are not happy with it, you can always change it later. Make sure you have at least 3 to 5 characters in your username, but do not use other symbols, punctuation marks, or dashes. Enter the required details and click "Create Account" to join Pinterest.

After your account is successfully created, you will be asked to "Follow 5 boards to get started." When you select a board or category that is shown on the left side of your screen, you will see the latest updates whenever you visit Pinterest. You can choose more than 5 categories. Click "Next" on the top of the screen to proceed to the next step.

How to Create a Board

To create your own board, click the "Add+" tab on your home page and select "Create a Board." Choose a unique name for your board and select the most appropriate category to which it belongs. You also have the choice to make your board secret. Additionally, pins you add to a secret board will not show up on Pinterest. This includes search results, your followers' home feed, your own home feed, or activity profile. Pinterest gives you a chance to create 3 secret boards, and they can be found at the bottom of your profile.

There is an interesting option titled, "Who can pin?" This basically decides who else can pin on your board. Simply enter the name or email address of the contributor and click "Invite."

As a board creator, only you have the permission to:

- Change the board title.

- Change the board description.

- Remove people from the board. However, people you invite can remove themselves directly.

- Delete pins from the board.

- If you follow any board, you can see all the pins that have been added to it right on your home page.

How to Add a Pin

A pin is an image or video you add to your Pinterest account. You can add a pin directly from a website or upload an image from your computer. To add a pin directly from a website, go to http://about.pinterest.com/goodies and scroll down the screen. Select "Pin It" and drag it to your browser's toolbar.

Select the image you would like to pin on your favorite website and click "Pin It" on your toolbar. You will have to select the board you want this image to feature, and you can also add a description. If you want your friends to know about it, you can also share the image on Facebook or Twitter.

Another way you can add pins from a website is using the "Add+" button. Click "Add+" on your home page and select "Add a Pin." Enter the website URL, choose a board, write a description, and click "Pin It."

To upload a pin directly from your computer, click the "Add+" button from your home page. Select "Upload a Pin" and select a file from your computer. Decide the board you'll pin to and, finally, add a description. Click "Pin It" once you are done. You can only pin images in JPEG, PNG, or GIF formats.

Pinterest Ads - Promoted Pins

Pinterest Ads' new feature, Promoted Pins, is their advertising option. Promoted Pins gives you the option to bring more visibility to the pins you have posted on your Pinterest page. Here is how it works:

- Sign up at https://ads.pinterest.com/
- Pick a Pin - Promote your best Pins so they appear in relevant search results.
- Decide who sees it - Set up targeting so the right people see your Promoted Pin.
- Pay for visits – You will only pay when people click through to your website.
- Track what's working - Once your campaign starts, see how it is doing and make changes.

Pinterest Analytics

With Pinterest Analytics, see what people like from your Pinterest profile and what they save from your website. Also, get new data about your audience so you can learn what your customers really want. You will also get advice on how to increase impressions, clicks, and Repins so you can refine your Pinterest strategy and reach more people.

When you login to your Pinterest account and go to https://analytics.pinterest.com/, you will see three key areas that are the basis of your Pinterest Analytics Data. The three areas are:

- Pinterest Profile - This tab gives you information on how people interact with pins on your Pinterest profile. Activity includes Impressions, Repins, Clicks, and All-Time combined data.

- Your Audience - This tab gives you monthly views, monthly engagement, countries, and cities that your users are coming from, languages they speak, and their gender.

- Activity from Website - This tab lets you know which pins people are Sharing, Liking, and engaging with from your website. Activity includes Impressions, Repins, Clicks, Original Pins, "Pin It" button usage, and more.

Tumblr and Blogs

Tumblr has become synonymous with the word, "blog," so much so that the term, "Tumblr," receives more searches on Google than "blog." We are seeing "blog" redefined and re-coined as we speak. Blogs were used to communicate more personally and intimately with online users before today's Social Media giants. However, there is still a place for blogs. Online users can subscribe to blogs via RSS feeds and stay updated via RSS readers or email. This subscription-based communication is a great way to maintain contact with a blog and a blogger with their subscribers. Organizations that have blogs (whether Tumblr or Wordpress) are opening up great ways for their online followers to stay connected. Many blogs are updated by CEOs and other members of leadership. This communication is a great way for online followers to feel more connected with the brand's leadership.

Key Tumblr Statistics

- There are +195 Million Tumblr Blogs.
- Around 120k users join Tumblr daily.
- There are 114 million Tumblr posts everyday, and there are 83.1 billion to date.
- Tumblr has around 200 million monthly visitors to their platform.
- 50% of Tumblr content is accessed via mobile devices.
- 61% of teenagers (13 - 19) consider Tumblr their favorite network.
- 14% of people 18-34 years of age use Tumblr.

How to Setup a Tumblr account:

Go to http://Tumblr.com and click the "Sign up" button at the top right. Enter your email address, password, and the username you would like to use on the Tumblr site. A good username would be the name of your organization or a shortened acronym of your organization. Tumblr wants you to get acclimated to what else is going on within their network, so they ask you to follow a few blogs to get comfortable.

You can check your Facebook friends or Gmail contacts to see if anyone you already know is on Tumblr. If your organization has a database of emails you want to connect with on Tumblr, you can import that database into Gmail contacts, search them from within Tumblr, and connect with them.

Now, you can post any of the update types that are in the top row, be they Text, Photo, Quote, Link, Chat, Audio, or Video. The purpose of Tumblr is not necessarily to always write a long post. You may compose longer posts, but the attention span of most people is very short these days. Therefore, a larger quantity of high-quality, short posts will yield much better results. Additionally, posting content, as well as engaging and following other users on Tumblr, will help increase your organization's presence.

Vine

Vine (http://vine.co) is a mobile Social Media platform owned by Twitter and is built on six-second videos. Estimates have it at 40 million users and growing. The app is available from the mobile app store for iOS, Android, and other devices. Users have found so many creative ways to create videos and build online audiences that they spend up to 12 hours filming a six-second clip. This platform has spawned a new group of online stars known as Vine Stars who are moving on to mainstream success simply because of their vine videos and their following. As you can imagine, this platform is here to stay. The audience for Vine is mainly teenagers and young adults, and its six-second videos appeal to the shrinking attention span of our culture.

One of the questions I am asked by many organizations is how they can utilize Vine, and whether they should even create an account. Here are two good thoughts to consider when it comes to using Vine: (1) Do you want to upload pre-created content or, (2) Do you want to distribute content recorded in-the-moment? Both types of content greatly affect audiences, and both can be an effective part of your Social Media content strategy. A great question to answer with Vine is how can you tell your organization's story in six-second moments. How can you get your viewers attention, hold it, and move them to action (Revine, Comment, Share on Twitter, or Like) in six seconds?

The platform is easy to use. You record videos with the "capture" button, or you can upload pre-recorded videos. You have a few editing options, such as cutting and slicing, then you publish the video to the platform. You can tag friends or other Vine users in the message you post with the video to alert them that they are in the post. Overall, Vine is a great platform that is growing in popularity, and its integration with Twitter is one of the best benefits.

Snapchat

Snapchat is one of the newest networks to come onto the scene and capture the attention of the younger demographic that has been leaving Facebook in droves. The short time span made it something that businesses and adults overlooked. The current key demographic for this platform is 13 - 25 years old, and here's the best part: They rarely logoff! The key feature of Snapchat is timed multimedia (photo and video) messages that are sent by a user to an entire or specified audience. Messages can be viewed within the range of a few seconds or for up to 24 hours. Snapchat also has a "Stories" feature where a user can connect a series of "snaps" (photos and videos) to tell a story.

With a short attention-span audience, such as the one that frequents Snapchat, there are a variety of different types of snaps that an organization can use to build an audience. Here are some key examples of great Snapchat content:

- Online Coupons - If you are having a sale, you can use this platform to send out an online coupon and let your subscribers go from online subscribers to revenue-generating customers.

- Behind-the-Scenes - One of the best features of Social Media is that it gives fans behind-the-scenes access to their favorite stars and brands. Snapchat is a great platform to give users quick glimpses of behind-the-scenes views and information on new products, events, or people.

- SnapCash - One of the best ways that Snapchat users are able to send money to each other is Snapcash. While this is no Paypal or online banking-killer, it is creating a new way for younger users to transfer finances between themselves. This leads to the question, "Will they continue to use these micropayment solutions in the future?"

Snapchat Ads

Snapchat Ads are a great feature because they have a very engaged audience. Snapchat, as a platform, has one of the most engaged audiences and resonates with younger people. The ads are not invasive. Therefore, the users that view ads will have actively engaged with your brand and made a choice to see your Snap Ad. As your organization continues to consider paid options, Snapchat is one to consider in the future. Similar to Instagram Ads, key information that could be gathered in Snapchat Ads that people view are location, demographics, phone type, data usage, and other relevant information.

Analyze, Optimize, Repeat

After you have implemented a great Social Media strategy and have seen people respond and interact with you on your networks, it is time to analyze your results, optimize your strategy, and repeat. Many organizations do not analyze their Social Media results. They take the "Just put it on Facebook or Twitter" approach and hope for the best. If your organization takes the time to develop a Social Media strategy, it should take the time to measure the results.

Analyze Your Results

In order to effectively measure Social Media results, you need to assess the following:

- How many people are seeing, Liking, and Sharing your posts on Facebook?
- How many people are Retweeting, Favoriting, and responding to your Tweets?
- What is the demographic of your online audience (age, sex, location)?
- How many people are following your Social Media links back to your website?
- How many people are clicking on the links you are posting?
- Who are your most important and influential followers?
- What social networks are sending the most people to your website(s)?

- How many Likes, Comments, and Regrams are you getting on Instagram?

- How many Repins, Likes, and Comments are you getting on Pinterest?

- How many Likes, Revines, and Comments are you getting on Vine?

- How many people are interacting with and Sharing your posts on Tumblr?

These stats are measured by the built-in analytics of the platform you are using and/or quite a few online software programs your organization should utilize. Whether it is Facebook Insights, Twitter Analytics, Hootsuite, SproutSocial, or another analytics platform, there is an abundance of ways to take this important data and turn it into useful information. The main point to understand is that it is absolutely necessary to measure the impact of your Social Media campaigns.

Optimize Your Strategy

Looking at your Social Media analytics and comparing the data of what you posted, when you posted, how often you posted, and which networks yielded which responses, we can look at ways to optimize your results. First, you want to see which times people responded to your posts. Next, you want to see which days garner the highest response. Additionally, as you optimize your strategy, you will want to continue creating and distributing visual content to your networks. Continue finding ways to create innovative and inspiring photos and videos that will engage your audience and compel them to share. If they are not Sharing, Liking, Retweeting, or Commenting enough, add more calls-to-action in your posts. Finally, utilize your hashtags on Twitter, Google+, and Instagram. Hashtags can help you create, get involved, and control conversations that occur about your organization and give you numerous opportunities to reach people.

<u>Repeat</u>

When you know better, you do better! Knowledge is power! Now that you have analyzed your results and optimized your strategy, it is time to repeat. Repeat the process of posting to your Social Media networks at the optimized times with the optimized content to achieve optimized results.

Social Media Commerce - Making Money via Social Media

The initial rise of social commerce, in my opinion, was a result of the social aspect of shopping. Shopping, in itself, has always been a social activity, whether it was people shopping together, a parent with a group of kids in tow, a spouse shopping for their entire family, or someone getting sales tips from a friend about products and services. Social Media made the shopping process even more social because, as we are able to shop offline or online, we can share our experiences with our friends via our chosen social networks. Take a look at these key statistics:

- 70% of marketers have been successful in gaining new customers via social networks.
- 57% of users trust more in the opinion of his/her contacts than in what the brand says about its product or service.
- 47% of social network users state that Facebook has had a bigger impact on their decision to buy than any other social network.

The early phase of social commerce was led by users sharing their shopping experiences with their networks, as well as companies providing social features to enhance the shopping experience. Enhancement included adding Social Media Sharing buttons to products and e-receipts so people could easily share these things. Amazon.com was one of the initial online stores to provide these features. Key networks on which these sharing features initially resonated were Facebook, Twitter, and Pinterest. Another example were offline stores providing Social Media advertising inside of their stores and on receipts, letting customers know these stores were active in the Social Media space. Once people connected to these companies online, they would receive incentives, such as online coupons and early sale notifications. The sharing of web links to online stores' coupons or websites was the key driver of early social commerce.

Fast forward to the current phase of social commerce. You will see it being led by the actual social networks. Certain social networks see the benefits, engagement wise and financially, of making the e-commerce process easier for consumers and sellers. Here are some of the key advancements in social commerce:

- Twitter Offers

  When users see a Twitter Offer in their timeline, they can add the offer to their credit or debit card in just a few taps, and redeem them in real time by using the card at the store. Because the offer is tied to their card, redemption is seamless and easy: there are no coupons to redeem at the point of purchase. After the purchase, the cash-back savings appear on their card statement within a few days.

With Twitter Offers, advertisers will be able to attribute redemptions directly to their campaigns on Twitter so they can effectively measure the ROI from their promotions, even when redemption happens offline. Additionally, we make it easy for merchants to get up and running. Because they can use their existing payment network, there is no change to the consumer purchase process, no employee training, and no new hardware or software to install. By leveraging Twitter's robust targeting capabilities, advertisers can tailor their promotions and campaigns to the right audience while optimizing for performance.

After users add a Twitter Offer to their credit or debit card, that card information will be encrypted and safely stored to make it easier for them to claim other offers or make purchases on Twitter in the future. We also give users the ability to remove this information from their account at anytime.

- Facebook Offers Button

    On your Facebook Fan page, you can click the "Create an Offer" option to create an online offer that people can redeem at a preset website. As you build the offer, you will be able to see exactly how it looks on users' screens. You choose a title for your offer, a description of your offer, upload or choose an image for people to see, choose a start and expiration date, how many people can claim this offer, and the website to which you are sending people to claim the offer. Once you have completed these steps, you can click "Create Offer."

- **Facebook Buy Button**

  With this feature, people on desktops or mobile devices can click the "Buy" call-to-action button on ads and page posts to purchase a product directly from a business all without leaving Facebook. Facebook built this feature with privacy in mind, taking steps to help make the payment experience safe and secure. None of the credit or debit card information people share with Facebook when completing a transaction will be shared with other advertisers, and people can select whether or not they would like to save payment information for future purchases.

- **YouTube Fan Funding**

  YouTube has a new feature called, "YouTube Fan Funding." This feature allows viewers to send voluntary payments to support the channels they love. To use this feature, your channel must be in good standing. Additionally, you must be a partner, have an AdSense account associated with your YouTube Channel, and have activated the feature in the creator studio channel section of our YouTube account. The money from your account is deposited into an associated Google Wallet account, which is Google's online payment feature.

- **Vimeo Tip Jar**

Vimeo Tip Jar enables Vimeo Plus and Vimeo Pro members to receive small cash payments from people who like their videos. It is a simple three-step process to enable Tip Jar. Step 1: Join Vimeo Plus or Vimeo Pro. Tip Jar is available only to Plus and Pro members. Step 2: Once you have signed up, connect your PayPal account. Step 3: Turn on Tip Jar for individual or all videos.

- <u>SnapCash</u>

  SnapCash is built upon the Square Cash platform. The sender and the recipient, however, are not associated with an email address, but a Snapchat ID.

  SnapCash is a really wonderful integration of the Square Cash platform, which utilizes the Debit Card network to simply send cash. The process to associate a Snapchat ID with SnapCash is almost precisely the same as Square Cash:

  - Once the sender registers a debit card associated with SnapCash, the sender simply types in the recipient's SnapChat ID for a stated amount.
  - The recipient will receive the message as a new notification and will either register a debit card to receive the funds, or accept the transaction onto a previously registered debit card.

There are two key social commerce options that are quickly rising. One is social shopping, and the other is social payments. The social payments option has seen much success in China with a number of chat/communication platforms integrated with payments. The key to making social buying a popular option will be to build great experiences around those buttons, because just placing buttons on social pages will not change habits. Currently, people do not associate social networks with shopping. They are more comfortable with leaving the social networks and going to the seller's website to purchase in a secure, online environment. If the social networks previously mentioned, as well as others, can create a cohesive online experience that integrates our online connections opinions/recommendations, a secure shopping process that keeps our financial information safe, and a shopping method that does not feel like it is more complex than a few clicks, social commerce will become wildly popular, especially via mobile devices because we are always connected.

Social Media and Sharing Everywhere

In addition to having a great visual content strategy and a great Social Media strategy, your organization should integrate Social Media Sharing features into all of your online properties. Very similar to the offline event experience where people share how great an event was with their friends once it is over, your website(s) should have Sharing features that allow people to Share their online experiences. On your homepage should be options to link to your Social Media websites. Likewise, people should be able to Share your website and the different pages they Like. If an online user Likes your business and wants to share your homepage with their Social Media friends, they should be able to! If an online user is watching an online video or live event and someone says something inspiring, they should be able to Share that event page with their Social Media Fans. Programmatically, there are ways to add these Sharing features to your website, and the easiest one we have seen is at ShareThis.com. From this website, you can add Sharing features for Facebook, Twitter, Pinterest, Google+, Email, and other Sharing methods.

Additional External Sharing Features

There are a variety of additional ways that Social Media can be integrated into your organization's marketing strategy to make sure people are able to stay connected online, even while they are experiencing offline events. The lines are blurring between online and offline. The more your organization is able to stay connected to your online users, even during offline events, the more your organization will have deeper Social Media connections with your Social Media Fans. Here are some examples:

- Marketing Materials – Add your Social Media pages to your marketing materials. No matter what it is, if your organization creates it and distributes it, make sure it has your Social Media channels on it. When people see your Social Media pages on marketing materials, they realize they can stay connected with your organization in a variety of ways.

- Leadership Buy-In – When the leader uses Social Media and guides the organization toward its use, there is a fundamental shift in the corporate culture. Customers see the organization embracing Social Media, and employees see this, too. This motivates employees to use Social Media internally, communicate with customers externally via Social Media channels and, thus, increase the online audience.

- Events – Offline events need an online component. I have worked with churches extensively, and during weekend services, there are some churches that do a great job of interacting with people via Social Media. New visitors are greeted when they tweet they are at the church or check in via Foursquare. The organization thanks them for coming and, sometimes, offers free gifts for letting the church know they were there. Likewise, during conferences, there are great examples of Social Media usage, such as adding hashtags to banners that are located throughout the conference. Letting attendees know the hashtag that represents the conference prior to them getting there allows them to market the conference via their social networks. Providing a page on their website that lets people Share conference content and information right from that website makes it easy for people to Share just by clicking on certain icons. Another great strategy I have seen for conferences is to have Google+ Hangouts with key speakers of the conference. This Hangout can be recorded and distributed via Social Networks. This type of video content generates interest in the event and provides potential attendees with Shareable content that can be viewed and Shared with their networks.

There are many more offline options that are available. Be creative and integrate Social Media into your marketing plans. Then, sit back and watch how interactive your online results can be.

<u>Social Media for Conferences</u>

One of the greatest aspects of conferences is the offline events that help create online conversations. When I am working with organizations that are planning conferences, I continue to remind them that, even though they are focused on the offline event and making it successful, they must not neglect the online aspect of the event and how it can impact the experience of virtual and actual attendees. When creating the online experience for the conference, we want to make sure the online experience enhances the experience of users at the conference as well as creates a great experience for users who are only participating online. This starts with four key areas: The web experience, the social experience, the mobile experience, and the streaming experience.

<u>Web Experience</u> - The web experience should be one that is:

- o <u>Easy to use</u> - The website should be easy to use, load quickly, and have a great layout. Build the website to suit the user, not the organization. The organization creates and populates the website. The users actually depend on and use it.

- o <u>Informational</u> - The website should be informational. Make it a destination of information. Key pages are speakers, schedule, topics, location, travel accommodations, and more.

o   Interactive - The website should be interactive, providing features that keep potential attendees coming back. Interactive features can be social (interactive Twitter feed, interactive Instagram feed, social Sharing links), and they can be informative, such as a news feed of latest conference updates. Keep users interested in your conference website by providing interactive features that encourage them to interact and Share your conference website.

Social Experience - The social experience is key to creating an interactive online audience. Here are some key things to consider:

o   Choose Key Social Media Networks - When you are looking at networks on which you want to promote your conference, you want to make sure you choose networks your audience already uses. Facebook, Twitter, and Instagram are ones that most organizations often use for adult audiences. When it comes to a younger demographic, they may forego Facebook for Vine or Snapchat. Make sure if you choose multiple networks, you have adequate staff to push updated, consistent content on these networks and interact with people in a timely manner.

o   Choose a Great Hashtag - A great hashtag can make or break the online aspect of a conference. If the hashtag is difficult to type and remember, the attendees will not use it, and neither will it gain traction. Without key traction, it makes the online aspect of the conference much more difficult to measure and promote. Choose a hashtag that is close to the title of the conference, a clever and short acronym of the conference, or a consistent, overarching theme of the conference that users can type quickly, Share easily, and remember.

o   Encourage and Facilitate Interactions - Sharing features on your website are a great start to facilitating social interactions about the conference. Giving people a way to Share your website, as well as prepopulating posts with text and hashtags, can help people Share with the simple click of a button. Additionally, when people are having conversations using the conference hashtag, interact with them from the official conference account. Retweet them and talk with them about the conference. Encourage them to Share, and make them feel like someone is listening to their excitement about this event. Do not forget to ask that speakers and presenters at the conference use the hashtag and Share the event with their online audiences as well.

<u>Mobile Experience</u> - Staying connected on-the-go is key to conference attendees these days.

o <u>The website needs to be a "responsive design"</u> so that it can be viewed on-the-go. Users are not sitting at desks and laptops that often at conferences, but they are carrying around mobile devices. Make sure your conference website is accessible and loads quickly on mobile devices.

o <u>A Conference app is better than a mobile website</u> - An even better option than a mobile website is a mobile app. Conference attendees are much more likely to download your conference app than go to your mobile website. This app gives the organization a much better connection to their users by using features such as push notification, real-time updates, and continued access after the event since the app is still installed on their device. Make sure your app has all the key pages from your website, social interactive features, and mobile streaming.

<u>Streaming Experience</u> - Watching the conference via live stream can be one of the most engaging aspects of the online experience.

o <u>Make video streaming adaptive</u> - Adaptive streaming means the video will adjust to the internet connection speed of the device. Whether the user is on a mobile

115

device with a slower connection or a desktop with high speed broadband, the stream will adapt to their connection and give them the best viewing experience.

o <u>Make the video HTML5 compatible</u> - HTML5 compatible video works on any device, and the best experience for the user is to make the video compatible on the device they choose.

o <u>Make desktop streaming interactive</u> - Whether it is an online live chat, a live, interactive Twitter feed, or a sharing button to promote the stream on social networks, make sure the desktop stream is interactive. There are a variety of options that can be added to the desktop streaming experience that can enhance it and increase engagement.

<u>Make Access Easy</u> - I cannot stress this enough! Make access to your conference's online properties easy. Users want a seamless online experience, or one very close to it. One of the most important aspects of the online experience is to promote it from offline venues. If there is a main stage or traditional marketing materials (goodie bags, flyers, etc.) that are given to attendees, make sure to inform them of the online aspects of the conference and ask them to "Stay Connected with us Online" while letting them know how (hashtag, mobile app, social networks, and more).

Where is Social Media going?

- <u>More Mobile Device Integration</u> – Right now, we see Social Media integrated into many aspects of our lives, and that will continue to grow. Facebook Home is a newly released platform that integrates Facebook very deeply into your Android Phone experience, basically putting your Social Media network front and center on the phone. This makes Social Media the main focus of the phone instead of the traditional emails, texts, and phone calls. This advancement shows how deeply integrated Social Media looks to become since millions of people carry their mobile devices with them. Social Media is looking to be the #1 use of your mobile device.

- <u>More Website Integration</u> – With Twitter cards now being more accessible via websites and the Facebook graph becoming more utilized, our social networks will play a role in our browsing and online usage. We will consult our social networks' opinions in our shopping, online decisions, and, therefore, make sure we are logged into our networks so that each website is catered to our Likes. Facebook and Google look primed to lead this evolution.

- <u>Share as much video as we do photos</u> – Right now, it is not as easy to share and consume videos like we do photos. Social networks and bandwidth restrictions make it much easier to share photos than video. Videos are increasing in consumption, but they do not have the volume of creation and distribution that photos and graphics currently have. As technology progresses and networks continue to focus on visual content, video will become just as important as photos.

- <u>Social media will continue to integrate into new industries</u> – Education and Health Care are two great examples of industries that are starting to use social features much more. This will continue to increase over time, and more industries will see the benefits of having social Sharing features more integrated into their online processes.

- <u>Social Networks on the Rise</u> – Pay attention to:
    - Secret.ly - Anonymous sharing platform
    - Shots.com – Selfies mobile social network app
    - WeChat.com - Mobile text and voice message service (strong international presence)
    - GoTinder.com - Mobile Dating app
    - Medium.com - Microblogging Platform
    - Whisper.sh - Anonymous sharing platform
    - Vessel.com - Original Content High Quality Video Platform

Conclusion

To summarize, your organization must evaluate and consider establishing a Social Media strategy, even if you start very small. The returns on your investment, in time, will be huge.

Thank You for Reading!

References

Twitter Offers - https://blog.twitter.com/2014/introducing-twitter-offers

Facebook Buy button - https://www.facebook.com/business/news/Discover-and-Buy-Products-on-Facebook-Test

YouTube Fan Funding - http://youtubecreator.blogspot.com/2014/06/look-ahead-creator-features-coming-to.html

Vimeo Tip Jar - https://vimeo.com/creatorservices/tipjar

Snapcash - http://blog.snapchat.com/post/102895720555/introducing-snapcash

Will Snapchat's Snapcash Be A Success? http://www.forbes.com/sites/quora/2014/11/26/will-snapchats-snapcash-be-a-success/

Mobile Social Media Stats - http://postcron.com/en/blog/social-media-trends-2014/

Sprout Social - http://sproutsocial.com/features/

Buffer - https://bufferapp.com/

Instagram - http://instagram.com/press/

Social Media Statistics - http://expandedramblings.com/

Pinterest - https://analytics.pinterest.com - https://business.pinterest.com/en/pinterest-analytics

Socialnomics - http://Socialnomics.net

Huffington Post - http://HuffingtonPost.com

YouTube - http://YouTube.com/ads

Twitter Analytics - https://analytics.twitter.com/about

http://www.fastcompany.com/3036184/how-to-be-a-success-at-everything/the-best-and-worst-times-to-post-on-social-media-infograph

Get additional books from Jason Caston at www.tenconnections.com. *Digital Connections* consists of the Five-Part Methodology to help organizations advance online. With a focus on Easy to Use Websites, Multimedia (Online Video and Streaming), eCommerce (Online donations and stores), Social Media and Mobile, these five parts can help your organization advance online. *Mobile Connections* consists of key mobile strategies and platforms to use when connecting with online users via their mobile devices. With a focus on mobile websites, mobile apps, mobile commerce, sms text, and much more, organizations can reach customers right where there are at any given time via their mobile devices.